BEAUTY ALL AROUND YOU

BEAUTY ALL AROUND YOU

How to Create Large Private Low-Maintenance Gardens, Even on Small Lots and Small Budgets

ROBERT GILLMORE

Photographs by Eileen Oktavec

Published by The Sant Bani Press
268 Main Street, Tilton, New Hampshire 03276
(603) 286-3114

Library of Congress Control Number: 00-133500
ISBN: 0-9701682-8-4

Printed in the United States of America
10 9 8 7 6 5 4 3 2 1

Cover Photograph: *See page 52.*

To Eileen

Books by Robert Gillmore

LANDSCAPE DESIGN

Beauty All Around You: How to Create Large Private Low-Maintenance Gardens, Even on Small Lots and Small Budgets (2000)

The Woodland Garden (1996)

GREAT WALKS GUIDES

Great Walks of Acadia National Park & Mount Desert (1990)

Great Walks of Southern Arizona (1991)

Great Walks of Big Bend National Park (1991)

Great Walks of the Great Smokies (1992)

Great Walks of Yosemite National Park (1993)

Great Walks of Sequoia & Kings Canyon National Parks (1994)

Great Walks of Acadia National Park & Mount Desert Island (1994)

Great Walks of the Olympic Peninsula (1999)

PUBLIC AFFAIRS

Liberalism and the Politics of Plunder: The Conscience of a Neo-Liberal (1987)

Contents

Acknowledgments

This book is an elaboration of ideas I first expressed briefly in an article, "The Art of Making Less Seem Like More," in the January/February 1966 edition of *Fine Gardening*, and in short sections of another book, *The Woodland Garden*, published by Taylor in 1966.

I am grateful to Taylor Publishing for permission to reprint photographs on pages 50, 53, and 55-60 and drawings on pages 23, 89, and 97.

I also want to express my thanks to my assistant, Claire Baker, for proofreading the manuscript with the same care with which she does everything else for me; to my agent, Robin Straus; to Diane Ryan for sensitively translating my rough sketches into excellent illustrations; and especially to my fiancee, Eileen Oktavec, for taking nearly all the photographs and drawing five of the illustrations in the book, for her careful reading of and astute comments on the manuscript, and for her constant support of my work. With much love, I dedicate this book to her.

ROBERT GILLMORE

Evergreen
Goffstown, New Hampshire
January 2000

With beauty before me...
beauty behind me...
beauty above me...
beauty below me...
beauty all around me...

— Navajo prayer

Introduction

New Landscaping for a New Landscape: Turning Your Yard into a Private Park

Think of the value of privacy. On a private lot, you don't see cars, trucks, and other people's houses. All you see is grass, trees, shrubs, flowers, and other growing things. Your home is a little green world where, in the vision of the Navajo prayer, beauty is all around you.

Privacy can also provide the most important characteristic of any landscape: unity. A landscape is unified when it's whole, when everything in it visually relates to—is in harmony with—everything else. A landscape is unified when, as Aristotle said of a work of art, nothing needs to be added and nothing needs to be taken away.

Unfortunately, the unity of your landscape can be broken by what's *outside* your property. For your landscape isn't only what you own; it's everything you can *see* from what you own. Your garden isn't just your lawn, trees, and flowers. It's also every house, road, sidewalk, telephone pole, and car that's visible from your home.

That point was poignantly, if inadvertently, made by a handsome older woman who one day offered to show me her garden. She led me to a large, well-groomed bed of colorful perennials along her front sidewalk. I looked down at the flowers. Then I looked at the line of houses, telephone poles, and cars up and down the street.

How sad, I thought. And how typical. The woman had lavished hours on her flowers—and her lawn and her shrubs—but had done nothing at all about the rest of her landscape. Like many homeowners, she had created a tiny island of beauty in an unsightly sea. She had gardened only a part of her landscape and forgotten the whole.

What is strange about this practice is that it's totally different from the way we decorate the inside of our houses. We don't paint one corner of a room and ignore the rest. We don't furnish that corner with a beautiful Queen Anne wing chair and use orange crates elsewhere. We decorate the entire space—everything we see. When we decorate our *outdoor* rooms, however, we're schizophrenic. We attend to just a few corners of the space and pretend that the rest of it doesn't matter.

The problem with development around our houses isn't only that it's so often unattractive. It's also that—attractive or not—the neighbors' houses simply don't "go" with our own landscape. The multihued green Victorian across the street, for example, doesn't harmonize with your gray Cape. Or it clashes with the brown contemporary beside it or with the yellow brick colonial on the other side.

Even if they were beautiful and harmonious, however, our neighbors' houses would still be intrusive, for they break one of the most useful rules of design: one space, one focal point. One strong visual element—a house, a sculpture, an imposing tree—can dramatically organize and unify a garden "room" or other area, but only when it's the *only* powerful visual component in the space. Add a strong competing element—another building, sculpture, etc.—and that unity is shattered; the power of one focal point is dissipated by the power of the other. Add still more powerful competing elements—several neighboring houses, for instance—and our attention is divided among so many competing focal points that the original simple unity becomes a visual Babel.

A private landscape is a unified landscape because its major focal point—its house—competes for attention with no other houses or other development. Standing alone, the house naturally dominates, organizes, and unifies its setting. Dominated by just one house—no more, no less—the landscape has visual integrity. Nothing needs to be added, nothing taken away.

The typical American home, of course, is anything but unified because it's anything but private. It's surrounded by other people's houses; by paved streets, driveways, and sidewalks; by traffic; by utility poles and overhead wires. And because the house is so close to the development around it, the sounds of nature are usually drowned out by the noise of civilization: the churning engines of cars, trucks, and motorcycles; the motors of lawn mowers, leaf blowers, weed whackers, and power saws; and by the unwelcome blast of neighbors' televisions, radios, tape decks, and electric guitars.

Two hundred years ago things were different. Most Americans lived in the country, on farms. Their houses were surrounded not by streets and other houses but by gardens, croplands, pastures, and woodlands that often stretched as far as their owners' eyes could see.

The internal-combustion engine had not been invented, so eighteenth-century Americans were spared the sight and sound of cars and trucks passing just a few yards from their houses.

The most elaborate transportation was a horse-drawn coach, so roads didn't need to be paved. Instead of looking at asphalt or concrete, early Americans saw only dirt roads. These "highways" were narrow and a bit rough, so they often looked more like wide paths than roads.

Because people were fewer and farther apart, "traffic" was light. Instead of a noisy car or van speeding by every few seconds, a horse pulling a wagon might come along every few hours. And far from being an annoyance, the horse, wagon, and driver might actually be a pleasing, welcome sight.

Because there was no electricity, no telephone or cable TV, no overhead wires cluttered the rural family's pastoral view of trees and sky.

Because there were no street lights, or no need for electric wires, there was no need to clutter roadsides with homely utility poles.

Nor was the eighteenth-century American ever bothered by noise from a neighbor's band saw, stereo, radio, or TV. In fact, his nearest neighbor was not only out of earshot but probably out of sight as well.

Thanks, in sum, to a relatively primitive, rural society, the typical early American lived in a large, peaceful, and nearly private landscape. He was surrounded not by houses and noisy streets but mainly by forests, pastures, croplands, and other growing things.

Over the last 200 years, however, most Americans lost their private pastoral landscapes. As they moved from farms to cities and towns they exchanged their forty-acre homesteads for half-acre lots, and their new houses were surrounded not by fields and woodlands but by paved streets and dozens of other houses.

Today, the private, rural, verdant residence that most Americans once took for granted is increasingly the privilege of the well-to-do. For with the ever-rising price of land, it's mainly the affluent few who can afford to build their houses on lots that are large enough to surround their dwellings with trees and meadows instead of other people's houses.

This problem, however, has a solution. While most of us can no longer afford ten or more acres, we can still afford privacy. For privacy doesn't require a lot of land. Even on small properties, privacy can be created with barriers, such as berms or hedges.

And just as privacy doesn't require 10-acre lots or 200-acre farmsteads, large green landscapes don't need to be orchards, meadows, and pastures, and they don't need to be vast flower beds and sprawling lawns that take countless hours to maintain. Just as there are other ways to create privacy, there are other ways to create large expanses of greenery. Gardens can be made of colorful trees, shrubs, ground covers, and other

Introduction: New Landscaping for a New Landscape:

plants that virtually take care of themselves.

The problem with our homes is not that they're on small lots and surrounded by other houses. It's that we're still landscaping them as if they were farms surrounded by fields and forests; as if the automobile had never been invented and our nearest neighbor were a mile away.

If we want to enjoy the landscapes that early Americans enjoyed, we can't landscape our homes as if they were farms or multiacre estates. We live in a more crowded world; our new landscape demands new landscaping. Since most of us can no longer have privacy automatically, we must *create* privacy. Since most of us can't afford a large rural, pastoral landscape or vast, expensive, high-maintenance gardens, we have to make large, inexpensive, low-maintenance gardens instead.

The great landscape architect Frederick Law Olmsted and his partner, Calvert Vaux, faced a similar challenge in the mid-nineteenth century. Millions of Americans had already moved into large cities, far from the pastoral scenery enjoyed by Americans who still lived on farms. Affluent city dwellers, of course, could afford country houses, or at least extended vacations away from the city. But ordinary city folk had no such escape. They were cut off from the natural scenery that other Americans could still take for granted.

Olmsted and Vaux's solution was both logical and radical: Since tenement dwellers couldn't afford to live in or even visit the country, the partners brought the country to the city. The most famous "country" they created was Central Park, which they transformed from a scruffy, swampy wasteland into an oasis of meadows, lakes, trees, and shrubs in the middle of New York City—a man-made but natural-looking 843 acres of countryside in the heart of one of the world's densest urban areas.

Olmsted and Vaux recognized that a new landscape required new landscaping—that changes in living conditions had to be matched by changes in landscape design. They realized that, if their generation of urban Americans were to enjoy the natural beauty that other Americans did, someone would literally have to create it.

Today we are at a similar crossroads. If we want to live in the large private landscapes that most Americans once lived in, then we must follow Olmsted and Vaux's example: We must use new means to achieve old ends. If we're not lucky enough to live in privacy, we must make privacy. If we're not already surrounded by natural beauty, we must build beauty. As Olmsted and Vaux transformed a large swath of mid-Manhattan into an oasis of natural scenery, so can we transform our own yards. As they turned parts of cities into parks, so we can turn our own homes into mini-parks.

How to Create Privacy . . .With Berms, Hedges, Fences, Walls, and Pergolas

Estates and other large properties get their privacy through the Daniel Boone method. According to legend, the storied frontiersman wanted his nearest neighbor to be at least a few miles away. When new settlers got too close, Boone would reclaim his precious "elbow room" simply by moving farther into the wilderness.

The affluent create privacy the same way Boone did. They don't need walls or solid fences. They can just build their houses far away from other people's houses, on large tracts of land often covered with lots of trees. Their land is at least several hundred feet deep and usually a lot more—so deep that they can't see any development around them. Their property is so large, and its trees so thick, that a solid fence or wall is unnecessary. The land and the trees *are* a wall.

Today most of us can't afford to create privacy the way Daniel Boone did. We have to do it much more efficiently, not with land but with hedges, fences, walls, pergolas, and—ideally—berms.

The Benefits of Berms

Berms are man-made but natural-looking ridges. They're usually made of fill, topped with loam, and planted with trees, shrubs, and other vegetation. Depending on the site, they can be made almost any height, width, and length. (See photographs on pages 49-53.)

A berm along the edge of your yard can block views of streets, cars, houses, and other development around your property. It can help create the same privacy that acres of land produce much less efficiently and much more expensively on large estates. Berms also enhance your sense of privacy by reducing noise from traffic, people, pets, TVs, and other noisemakers.

Hedges, masonry walls, and solid fences can provide screening too. But berms are the best screen of all, for all these reasons:

- Berms are solid, so they block views completely. Many hedges don't, because they have at least some space between their branches and leaves, and deciduous hedges, such as barberry or privet, lose most of their screening power when their leaves fall off. While fences can be built as solid as berms, they have disadvantages that berms don't (see below).

- Berms are denser than hedges and fences and thicker than walls, so they block sound better.

- Unlike hedges, fences, and walls, berms can be planted with trees and shrubs, which can provide even higher screening. Plus, the trees and shrubs can be planted in wide, thick clusters that create more solid screening than a typically narrower hedge.

- Berms can be made any height and still be attractive. (After all, they look just like a ridge or a little hill.) Plain fences and walls are apt to be eyesores if they're more than eight feet high. To be attractive, higher fences or walls have to be more elaborate (see page 27), and the extra detail makes them much pricier than simpler, factory-made six- or eight-foot fencing. And unlike a berm, even an elaborate fence or wall is unsightly if it's higher than a house or other building beside it.

- Because berms can be built higher than most fences and walls, they can block more of an unwanted view. An ordinary six- or eight-foot fence simply isn't tall enough to hide a building more than one story high. Berms, on the other hand, can be built high enough to screen virtually any single-family house.

- Hedges need pruning; fences need painting or staining and regular rebuilding; brick and stone walls need repointing. Berms, however, need no maintenance at all. After all, how could they wear out? They're dirt.

- Because berms don't wear out, they're the least expensive privacy barrier in the long run. Even in the short run, berms cost less than walls of equal height and about the same as hedges—which, again, are less effective barriers than berms. Only a fence is cheaper; but the liabilities of fences, plus their high maintenance cost—more than that of any other barrier—make them anything but a bargain.

☙ Berms are not just practical; properly shaped (see pages 22-23), they're interesting landforms. Their gentle hilly contours provide welcome relief from the sometimes monotonous floorlike flatness of a typical yard. Unlike fences, walls, or formal hedges, a well-designed berm looks natural. It looks great in a naturalistic garden. Fences and walls, on the other hand, are very obviously not natural.

☙ The slopes of berms are almost ideal platforms for displaying plants. On level surfaces, plants are often hidden by other plants in front of them. On berms, plants conceal much less, and sometimes nothing at all, of the plants behind them because they're higher up the slope. Because berms raise plants off the floor and up the walls of an outdoor room, they distribute plants more widely throughout the three dimensions of the garden, making it fuller and more lush.

☙ Some people think walls and fences are unfriendly and unneighborly. They certainly *are* unneighborly if they're homely and unattractive. Berms are different. They do the work of walls and solid fences—creating privacy—but they do it without the offensiveness of fences or walls—because, of course, they don't *look* like fences or walls. Walls and solid fences are tall, flat, vertical, sometimes unsightly, and obviously man-made barriers that, not surprisingly, *look* like privacy barriers. Berms, on the other hand, are subtle. They don't look like barriers. Properly designed and planted (see pages 74-75), they look like what they are: graceful landforms lushly planted with handsome evergreen trees and shrubs. Unlike fences and walls, berms are *very* neighborly. For what is unneighborly about a handsome planting of trees and shrubs? In fact, isn't a front yard with lots of trees and shrubs usually more interesting and more beautiful than a front yard planted with little more than a large flat lawn?

☙ Walls and fences have another disadvantage: In many communities they're illegal if they're more than a certain height or too close to the street or property boundary. Berms are usually unregulated, because they don't need to be;

they're not offensive. You can build them high enough to provide as much screening as you need.

Berms do, however, have one potential disadvantage: Unlike other privacy barriers, a berm must be at least twice as wide at its base as it is high. A three-foot-high berm, for example, has to be at least six feet thick at the bottom, six-foot berms at least twelve feet wide, and so forth. That's because, when you dump a pile of earth on the ground, it falls in a roughly pyramidal shape. The slope of the pile is known as the "angle of repose." That's the angle that earth will assume when it falls freely and comes to rest, or "repose," without any kind of retainer or support. The typical angle of repose is about forty-five degrees. When a pile of dirt rests at that angle, the bottom of the pile is exactly twice as wide as the height of the pile.

To be attractive, the slope of a berm should be a bit gentler, or less steep, than the angle of repose, so the base of a berm should actually be slightly wider than twice its height.

The space taken up by a berm isn't a problem because the space is "lost." The space, of course, is not lost—it's still there. The bottom of it is just graded into a different (hillier) shape. Actually a berm has *more* space—more surface area—than flat ground does, because sloping land has more surface area per acre than level land (see Figure 1). And just like any slope—or nearly any other part of your land, for that matter—a berm can (and, indeed, should be) planted with trees, shrubs, and ground covers. In fact (as noted above), it's an excellent showcase for plants.

A berm is a problem only when it takes up space needed for a patio, play area, or other outdoor amenity. Some house lots— many city properties, for instance—are so small that the whole yard may be needed for outdoor living areas. If a lot is too small for a berm, you'll need narrower barriers. (To see how much space you have or will have for privacy barriers, consult the checklist of outdoor amenities on page 28.

Room taken up by a berm on your property can be reduced if you can convince your neighbor to allow at least some of it to spill over onto his or her land. You can remind him that a berm will benefit both of you because it will create privacy for you *and* him. (If he hasn't thought about the value of privacy before, lend him a copy of this book!) If he likes the idea of privacy as much as you do, he may even offer

How to Create Privacy . . .

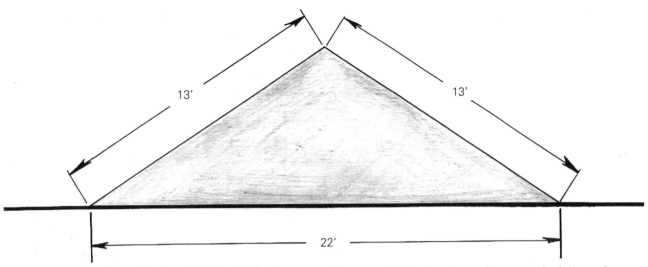

FIGURE 1: *Space taken up by a berm isn't "lost." On the contrary, a berm actually <u>adds</u> space to a garden, because the sloping surface area of a berm is larger than the area of the ground underneath the berm. The surface of this berm, for instance, is twenty-six feet wide, while the ground below it is only twenty-two feet wide.*

to share the cost of the berm.

You and your neighbor could also negotiate for what each of you wants more. If, for example, he has plenty of room, he might allow all or most of the berm to be built on his land in exchange for your paying all or most of its cost.

If your neighbor isn't as enthusiastic about a berm as you are, you might offer to pay him to allow a certain amount of it to be built on his land. You might also offer to incorporate some of his wishes (if any) about the shape of the berm or the plantings on his side of it. As with any negotiation, think of what you want most from your neighbor and what he might want in return.

On pages 19-27 I explain how to build berms. On pages 27-28 I discuss hedges, fences, walls, and pergolas. Before you decide what kinds of privacy barriers you need, however, you have to decide how high they should be and where they should be built.

Determining the Height and Location of Privacy Barriers

If your property is typical, it's surrounded by other houses. If your lot is typical—an acre or less—you can see those

houses (and other development) from almost anywhere on your land. If so, you'll need barriers all around your lot.

Some homeowners are lucky: Instead of houses, they have deep woods or other natural features on one or more sides of their property. If you're one of those fortunate few, you can "borrow" scenery (see pages 89-90) instead of hiding it. You'll need fewer barriers, or perhaps none at all.

Most houselots, however, need at least some screening on every side, and especially along the street, where the scenery is almost certainly development, not nature.

Determining where a barrier should go involves not one decision but two. First you decide that a barrier should be erected somewhere along an imaginary straight line that runs from the spot where you're standing to the development you want to block (Figure 2). Then you decide exactly *where* along that imaginary line you should erect the barrier.

In most cases, the barrier should go on the edge of your property, leaving you with the largest amount of private land.

Sometimes, however, a barrier should be nearer the center of your property. For example, if some or all of your boundary is lower than the rest of your lot, or your neigh-

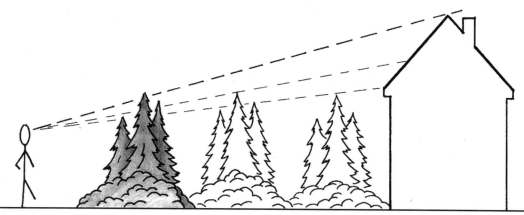

FIGURE 2: *A privacy barrier can be erected anywhere along a straight but imaginary line that extends from your viewpoint to the house or other development you want to block. To screen the house completely, the barrier must be as high as the imaginary line. The closer the barrier is to the house, the higher it has to be.*

bor's lot, or both, then a barrier on the boundary might not block *any* views (see Figure 3). In that case, the barrier has to be built on higher land, nearer the middle of your property (Figure 4). The land outside the barrier won't be private; but it's still the best choice, because a little less private space is much better than no privacy at all.

After you decide where a barrier should be built, you have to figure out how high it should be. You can estimate the height by imagining a straight line running directly from your eyes to the top of the object or objects you need to screen. To screen the object completely, the top of the barrier must be high enough to reach the imaginary line (Figure 4).

The higher the place you're standing on, the higher the barrier must be (Figure 5). To make sure your barrier will be high enough, estimate the height it has to be from various places on your land, including the highest points on your lot. Don't forget views from inside your house.

If you want, you can measure exactly how high a barrier must be. Here's how: Get a bamboo pole or similar object that's at least as long as a barrier needs to be high. (You may have to lash two poles together to make one long enough.) Paint the pole with brightly colored rings, one foot apart. Stick the pole in the ground wherever you need to build a barrier, or have someone hold it in place. Note the point on the pole that appears to be the same height as the object you

want to screen (Figure 6). Then count the total number of rings between that point and the ground. That number (minus the distance, if any, that the pole is stuck in the ground) is the number of feet your barrier must be to screen the object from view at the place you're standing. Repeat this process at other places on your lot to make sure your barrier will be high enough to hide the object at those points too.

In general, the lower the houses in a neighborhood and the farther apart they are, the lower the privacy barrier can be.

Houses on large country lots can obtain privacy with relatively low barriers and houses on small city lots need higher ones. But virtually every suburban lot and even many city lots—even plots as small as a quarter-acre—can be screened entirely with planted berms.

That's because the houses on these lots are usually single-family dwellings no more than two stories high, their lots are usually at least one-hundred feet wide—wide enough for berms—and the tallest development they need to screen are other two-story houses, which are usually less than twenty-five feet high. Since a barrier rarely has to be higher than the object it screens (and can usually be a few feet lower), most two-story houses can create privacy with berms or berm-and-evergreen barriers less than twenty-five feet high.

How to Create Privacy . . .

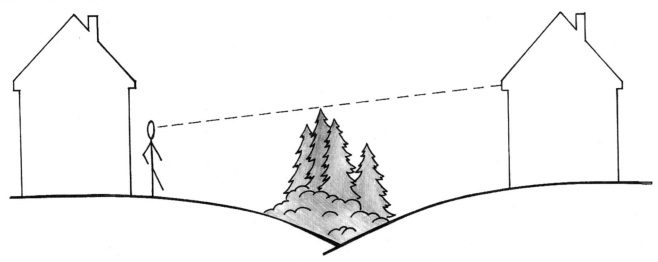

FIGURE 3: *Privacy barriers are usually built near the property line. But if the boundary is a low spot, a barrier there might screen nothing.*

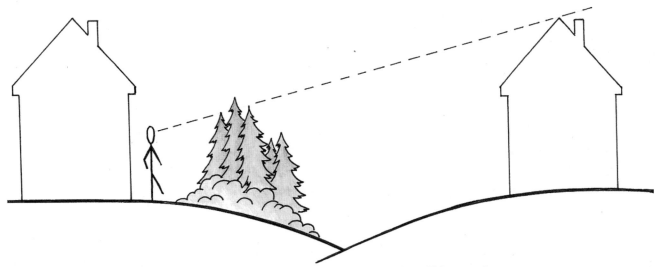

FIGURE 4: *If the property line is in a low place, a privacy barrier may have to be built on higher ground.*

How to Build Berms

Berms are easy to build. Simply dump fill on the ground, grade it into the shape you want, cover it with a layer of loam, rake it smooth, and plant it.

The best fill has two characteristics: It's stable—it won't move or wash away—and it will allow water to drain through it. Good fill is a mixture of clay, which provides stability, and sand or gravel (whichever is cheaper), which allows drainage. A berm is also a fine place to bury any rocks, brush, or other nontoxic debris you want to get rid of.

The loam should be deep enough to accommodate the root balls of whatever trees or shrubs you plant on the

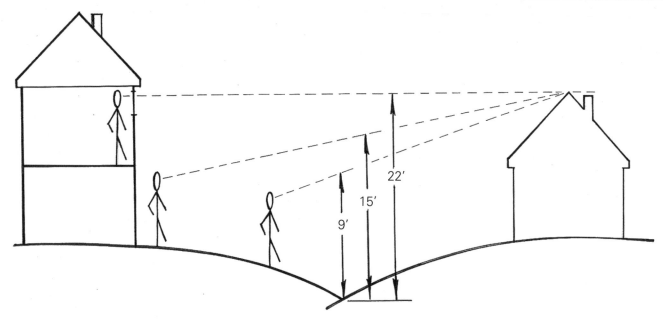

FIGURE 5: *The higher your viewpoint, the higher a privacy barrier has to be. To block a view of a neighbor's residence from the second-story window of this house, the barrier must be about twenty-two feet high. To block the same view from the grounds or the first floor of the house, the barrier has to be only fifteen feet high. A nine-foot barrier will block the view from a low spot.*

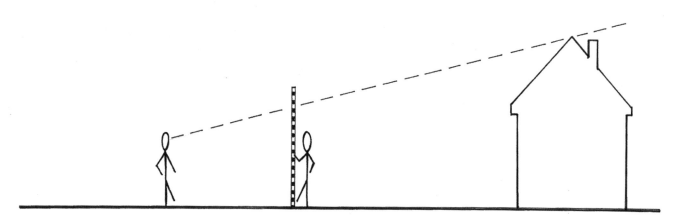

FIGURE 6: *To measure exactly how high a privacy barrier must be, use a long pole, marked off in one-foot sections, where the barrier will be built.*

How to Create Privacy . . .

berm—at least a foot for shrubs, one to two feet for trees.

A landscape contractor or other supplier can figure out how many cubic yards of loam or fill you'll need to build a berm. If you want to estimate the amount yourself, check the box below.

Since most yards are accessible to heavy equipment, dump trucks can haul in the fill and loam, and a backhoe or similar machine can shape the fill and spread out the loam. You can mark the ground with stakes or surveyor's tape to show the truck driver exactly where to dump the fill, and you can tell the backhoe operator exactly how you want the berm shaped (discussed on pages 22-23).

Have the backhoe operator make both the fill and the loam as even as possible; then make them even smoother by raking them by hand. The head of a landscaper's rake, incidentally, is about three times as wide as the head of an ordinary iron rake, so it does the job much faster and makes the earth more even; consider buying, borrowing, or renting one.

You can do some shaping, if necessary, when you rake. If the berm is too steep in some places, for instance, rake the fill or loam from the top of the berm toward the bottom. (Rake downhill whenever you can, because gravity helps you move the dirt and makes the work easier.)

If the site is steep or surrounded by large rocks or trees, or is otherwise inaccessible to heavy machinery, construction is more difficult. In that case you can carry the dirt to the berm site in a wheelbarrow and grade the berm with a shovel and rake, or you can make the site accessible to machinery by building a very rough access road—just smooth enough and wide enough for equipment to pass. A dump truck, for example, is about ten feet wide, a pick-up truck about eight feet, a backhoe or bulldozer about nine feet, and a Bobcat about six feet.

There are pros and cons for either building an access road or carrying the dirt in a wheelbarrow. An access road

How To Figure Out How Much Fill and Loam a Berm Will Need

First decide how high, how long, and how wide you want your berm to be and roughly how steeply it should be sloped.

Then decide how deep a layer of loam you need. (A typical *average* depth is one foot.)

Suppose your berm will be a total of 4 feet high on its crest, or highest point, and 10 feet wide and 40 feet long at its base, with 1 foot of loam on the top. To figure out how much fill you'll need, first subtract the depth of the loam (1 foot) from the total height of the berm (4 feet). That gives you the total height of the fill—3 feet. Then double the depth of the loam (1 foot x 2, or 2 feet) and subtract that amount from the width of the berm (10 feet). That gives you the total width of the fill—8 feet. Then subtract the doubled depth of the loam (2 feet) from the length of the berm (40 feet). That gives you the total length of the fill—38 feet. Then multiply the height of the fill (3 feet) by half its width (4 feet) and multiply that result (12 feet) by the length of the fill (38 feet). That gives you the total number of cubic feet of fill—456—that you need. To convert that amount to cubic yards (the way fill and loam are sold) divide it by 27, which is the number of cubic feet in a cubic yard (456 divided by 27 equals 16.88 cubic yards).

To figure out *approximately* how much loam you need, take the width of the berm (10 feet) and add 20 percent (2 feet), which gives you 12 feet. That's roughly the width of the berm *on its surface*. Now multiply the surface width (12 feet) by the length (40 feet), which gives you the surface area (480 square feet). Then multiply the area by the depth of the loam (1 foot). That gives you the total volume—480 cubic feet—of loam you need. To convert that amount to cubic yards, divide by 27 (which gives you 17.77 cubic yards).

If you want to determine *exactly* the volume of loam you need, the formula is:

$$2\sqrt{H^2 + \left(\frac{W}{2}\right)^2} \times L \times D = V$$

H is the height of the berm, W the width, L the length, D the depth, and V the volume. The formula gives you 512.24 cubic feet or 18.97 cubic yards—close to the approximate amount, which was computed without having to square numbers or to calculate square roots.

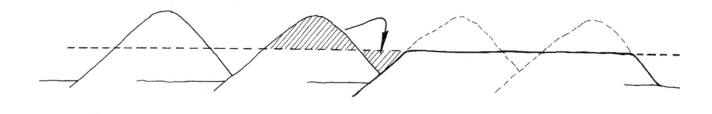

FIGURE 7: *If a dump truck driver drops each load of loam as close as possible to the previous one, he or she can almost build a (low) berm for you—without using a backhoe or any other machinery. Simply smooth out the berm by shoveling or raking loam off the top of the piles into the valleys between them.*

is an additional expense, and in building it you might have to destroy some valuable trees or other natural features. On the other hand, wheelbarrowing dirt is hard, slow work. And the higher the berm, of course, the longer the work will take. Then again, it's also unskilled work, and you can almost certainly hire people (local high school or college students, for example) to help you do it at modest wages.

Happily, the boundaries of most properties *are* accessible to heavy equipment, so most berms can be built mechanically. Only the final grooming has to be done by hand.

Other than plants, of course, loam is the most expensive part of a berm. Paradoxically, however, small, low berms—those less than three or four feet high—can often be built most economically by loam alone. This is why: When a ten-yard dump truck drops its load, the pile will be three or four feet high—as tall as a low berm. If you tell the driver to dump each load as close as he can to the previous load (see Figure 7), he can, in effect, almost build the berm for you. The tight row of piles will be so much like the final shape of the berm that you'll be able to finish grading it with just a shovel and rake. Mainly you'll have to scrape loam off the tops of the piles and spread it into the valleys between them.

By using just loam, you won't need to hire a backhoe to spread a couple of feet of fill and then a foot of loam on top of it. The only heavy equipment you'll need is the dump truck that delivers the loam. And the money you'll save by not hiring a backhoe, at $50 or more per hour, will often exceed the higher cost of building a berm entirely of loam.

Here's another way to save money: Unscreened loam is always cheaper than screened loam. If the unscreened soil contains only a few rocks, sticks, and other debris, it's often better to use it. That's especially true if you're building berms out of loam alone, because most of the debris will remain hidden, well below the roots of anything planted above it. The little labor required to pick up a few unsightly branches on the surface of the berm is usually justified by the lower cost of unscreened loam.

If all a berm had to do was block unwelcome views and noises, it could literally be nothing more than a pile of dirt. But a berm must be more than utilitarian. It also has to look natural, as if it had been there all along. It should look not like a pile of earth dumped *on* the site, but like a natural part *of* the site.

Make sure the berm doesn't look like a wedge: knife-edged at the top, flat on the sides, and straight from end to end (see Figure 8). A berm should resemble a natural ridge. Its crest should be rounded, and it should undulate at least a little, rolling up from cols to peaks and back down again. Some of its slopes should be gentler than others, and they could include both spurs and creases. The entire berm should curve irregularly from end to end (see Figure 9).

How to Create Privacy...

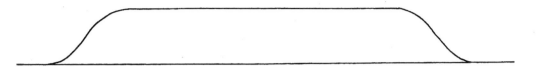

FIGURE 8: *Don't build a berm like this—flat on the top and sides and straight from end to end.*

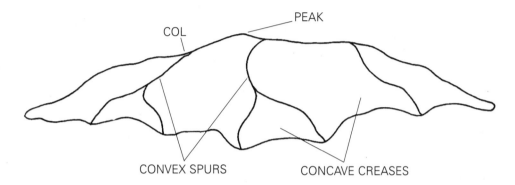

COL

PEAK

CONVEX SPURS

CONCAVE CREASES

FIGURE 9: *Instead, shape it like a natural ridge. The crest should be rounded, and it should undulate at least a little, rolling up from cols to peaks and back down again. Some of the slopes should be gentler than others, and they could include both (convex) spurs and (concave) creases.*

Berms are rarely subject to erosion, even before they're planted. Usually rain simply drains into the earth where it falls. To make sure you don't have problems, however, make the slopes at least a few degrees gentler than the angle of repose (explained on page 16). The closer the angle of a slope is to the angle of repose—in other words, the steeper the slope is—the more unstable it will be; the smaller the angle of the slope—that is, the more nearly level it is—the more stable it will be. (And, incidentally, the easier it will be to plant.)

Also be sure that there are no deep or steep depressions where water can make gullies. If gullies do appear, fill them in and/or smooth them out with a rake.

On many properties, a berm can't run uninterrupted along the entire length of the boundary; it has to be broken up by a driveway or walkway. But if the berm is interrupted—if it simply stops on each side of a driveway or

walk—then the property won't be completely private: you'll be able to see through the opening where the driveway or sidewalk is (see Figure 10). To block this opening, you can overlap the ends of the berm (Figure 11).

If you can't make the ends of the berms long enough to create all the screening you want, you can build a saddle—a low pass or rise between the ends of the berm—and route the driveway or walkway on top of it. Saddles are miniberms, or little berms between big berms (Figure 12).

Unfortunately, saddles usually can't be made as high as typical berms, because their slopes can't be as steep as those of the usual berm—they have to be gentle enough for a walkway or driveway. The more gradual slopes mean that the base of a saddle must be much wider than the base of a berm of equal height. (Berms can be just two or three feet wide for every foot of height, while saddles must be at least six feet wide.) If space is limited, the width, and therefore the height, of a saddle will be too (Figure 12).

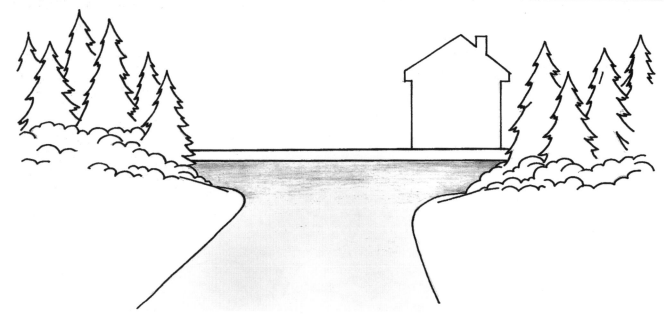

FIGURE 10: *If a berm must be interrupted to allow a driveway or sidewalk to pass through it, the property won't be completely private.*

FIGURE 11: *To block the opening, you can overlap the ends of the berm.*

How to Create Privacy . . .

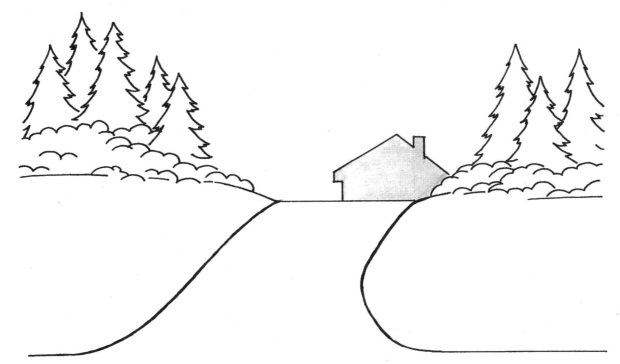

FIGURE 12: *If overlapping the ends of the berms still doesn't create enough privacy, you can build a saddle between the ends.*

FIGURE 13: *If you can't make a saddle high enough to block a view completely, you can install a gate at the saddle's highest point.*

. . . With Berms, Hedges, Fences, Walls, and Pergolas   25

If neither a saddle nor the overlapping ends of the berms create enough privacy, you can install a solid gate at the highest point of the saddle (Figure 13).

If you have to build a berm over the roots of a tree, you'll have to determine whether the berm would kill the tree and, if so, whether the tree is worth trying to save. Ideally, the ground beneath a tree should be undisturbed all the way from its trunk to its drip line, which is the widest spread of its foliage. If too much of this ground is covered with too much dirt, the roots of the tree, which are inside the drip line, will not get enough water and air, and the tree will die. If you cover only half of the roots with only a few inches of topsoil, a healthy tree will probably survive. But if you cover all the roots with a foot of topsoil the tree's life will be precarious. If you cover all the roots with, say, three or more feet of topsoil, the tree is almost certainly doomed.

Whether a berm-endangered tree deserves special consideration depends, of course, on the tree. A large, healthy, colorful dogwood or maple, for example, is much more valuable than a small cherry or ash. Still more valuable is a large, healthy, handsome evergreen that provides not only beauty but—more important—year-round screening. It's an unhappy irony if one privacy barrier has to be destroyed in order to create another.

There are several possible solutions. One is simply to route a berm away from a valuable tree. Another is to move it *slightly* away, so only a little bit of earth—no more than a

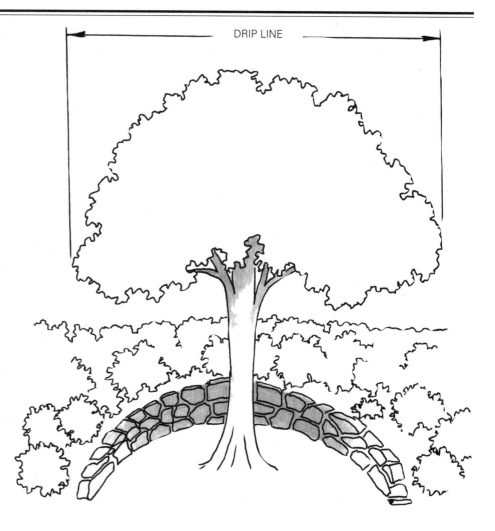

FIGURE 14: *A tree well can protect a tree by keeping earth away from at least some of the ground beneath its branches.*

foot—spills under the drip line. You can also keep a berm away from the tree by making the slope of the berm steeper than usual; just take care to disguise the steepness with evergreen plantings.

Trees can also be saved by a tree well, which is simply a stone wall built around a tree to keep soil away from it (Figure 14.) A tree well can be a handsome addition to a garden; sometimes it doubles as a bench, and plants look wonderful climbing up or spilling over it. Like most walls, however, tree wells are pricy, labor-intensive infrastructure.

Still another solution is to install a network of perforated pipes above a tree's roots. The pipes are designed to bring the roots both air and water. This procedure, however, is best done by a professional arborist, and it's not always effective, especially if the roots are covered with several feet of dirt.

What you do (or don't do) to save a tree will depend on its value—as a source of color, as a privacy barrier, and so forth—and on your budget.

After the berm is finally installed and shaped, it's ready to be planted. (See pages 74-75.)

Creating Privacy with Hedges, Fences, Walls, and Pergolas

Many homes, especially in cities, are on small lots— usually less than a quarter-acre (no more than one-hundred feet square) and typically only a fraction of that. Many of these houses are three or more stories high—they're typically multifamily dwellings—and they're usually close to other multi-story houses, also on small lots. Often these buildings are only a few feet away from each other. To attain complete privacy, they need higher privacy barriers than any other houses. Unfortunately, they have the smallest amount of land on which to build them.

These homes usually have room for only small berms, if any, and certainly not enough space for berms high enough to create complete privacy. But if they can't create privacy with berms, they *can* create it with hedges, walls, fences, or pergolas.

After berms, evergreen hedges are the most valuable privacy screen. They grow higher than most fences or walls, so they can provide more screening than either one. Unlike fences or walls, they need virtually no maintenance. They're also less expensive than walls, and they're softer, friendlier, and more natural-looking barriers than fences *and* walls. (Evergreen trees and shrubs for privacy barriers are discussed on pages 38-40, 46-48, and 61-63. Planting hedges is described on page 75.)

Even narrow, columnar evergreens (see page 40) can grow ten to twelve feet wide at maturity, however, and some (typi-

cally urban) lots simply don't have enough room for them. Those properties have to use even narrower privacy barriers: walls or wooden fences.

If you need to create privacy with fences or walls, keep these things in mind:

☙ A fence or wall is a bit of architecture, which should harmonize with the major architecture on the site: your house. A fence or wall usually looks best if it looks like an extension of the house, even if it doesn't actually touch it. Ideally, it should match both the colors and materials of your house. A white clapboard house should have a white clapboard fence; a red-brick house should have a red-brick wall, a field-stone house a field-stone wall, and so forth.

If a fence or wall made of identical materials is too expensive for your budget, at least its color can harmonize with your house. A white-painted house, for example, should probably have a white-painted fence; a brown-stained house should have a brown-stained fence. A stone or brick house would look good with a fence painted the same color as the shutters. The house trim or door or shutter colors should also match the trim colors of the fence, if any. Board fences, by the way, go better with most houses than stockade fences do. The latter go with almost no buildings at all.

☙ The ideal fence or wall is high enough to provide complete privacy but not so high that it's an eyesore. The more attractive, more interesting, and more complex a fence or wall is, the higher it can be. A plain, factory-made eight-foot-high board fence, for example, can look fine topped with four-foot lattice and provide a total of twelve feet of screening. A handsome clapboard or shingle fence that matches the house beside it can be as tall as the side of the house.

Remember, however, that many communities restrict the height of walls and fences, and sometimes other aspects too. Be sure to check before you build.

In urban areas, even a high fence or wall will probably not screen multistory buildings completely. In that case, however, you can build a pergola over some or all of the outdoor space (see Figure 15).

A pergola is a kind of open ceiling for an outdoor room. It's usually made of a parallel overhead joists, usually two-by-

FIGURE 15: *A pergola can create privacy on small, urban lots, where neighboring buildings are usually too tall to be screened by fences or walls alone. Planted with vines and surrounded by a fence or wall, a pergola can be the ceiling of a private outdoor room.*

six or two-by-eight-inch boards. The joists are supported by beams, usually two-by-eight-inch boards. The beams, in turn, are supported by posts, typically four-by-four-inch or six-by-six-inch timbers. Planted with climbing vines, a pergola provides not only light shade but substantial privacy to anyone beneath it.

By combining a fence or wall and a pergola, you can screen out almost all views of other buildings, even in a city. If you build a wall or fence all the way around the space you want to enclose, and if you build a pergola across the entire length and width of the space, and if the fence or wall reaches all the way up to the height of the pergola, then the pergola becomes the ceiling, and the wall or fence becomes the walls of an outdoor room (see Figure 15).

Checklist of Outdoor Amenities

To decide what kinds of privacy barriers are right for your property, you must first determine how much space you'll have available to build them. Decide which of these possible outdoor amenities (if any) you want to add to your yard:

- Terrace.
- Fireplace, barbecue, or other built-in outdoor cooking facility.
- Swimming pool, hot tub, and/or spa.
- Poolhouse or cabana.
- Children's special play areas, including sandboxes, swing sets, etc.
- Paved surfaces for tennis, basketball, shuffleboard, or other games.
- Soft surfaces such as grass for volleyball, badminton, horseshoes, croquet, etc.
- Pen or run for dogs or other pets.
- Vegetable or flower garden, fruit trees or bushes.
- Greenhouse, garden shed, and storage buildings, including places to store firewood, trash cans, garden supplies, boats, recreational vehicles, and other large items.

You won't want everything on this list. In fact, you

How to Create Privacy . . .

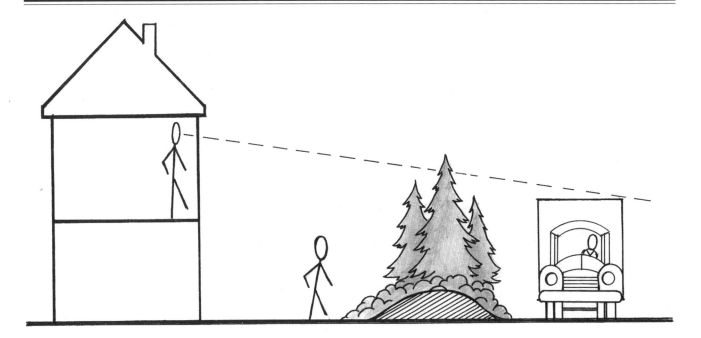

FIGURE 16: *House No. 1 can completely block any view of development from any point on its property—including second-story windows—with only a thirteen-foot-high barrier along the edge of the road.*

may already have everything or nearly everything you want or realistically hope to have. Some things, such as your lawn, you may want to make smaller (see pages 82-83). After you've decided what you plan to add, determine where they'll go and how much space they'll take. Then you can see how much space is left for privacy barriers.

To get an idea of how tall a barrier you'll need to screen your property from development, compare your home with the properties below.

1. A two-story house on a one-acre lot (about 600 feet wide by 700 feet deep), bordered on three sides by undeveloped woodlands and on the fourth side by a public road (Figure 16).

The only development the owners of this house can see is the road and, of course, passing cars and trucks; so all they need for complete privacy is a relatively low barrier along the road.

A seven-foot-high barrier would block views of the road and cars from any place on the grounds and from any window on the first floor of the house. A ten-foot barrier would screen big trucks from the same viewpoints.

A nine-foot barrier would screen views of the road and cars from the second-story windows—the highest viewpoints on the property—and a thirteen-foot barrier would hide large trucks.

This property has more than enough land to permit all the privacy barriers to be berms.

A thirteen-foot-high berm would completely block any view of development from any place on the property and substantially reduce traffic noise.

If, for some reason, the owners wanted a smaller berm, they could make their thirteen-foot barrier a combination of a berm and evergreen trees or shrubs planted on top of it. They could, for instance, build an eight-foot berm and plant it with five-foot trees.

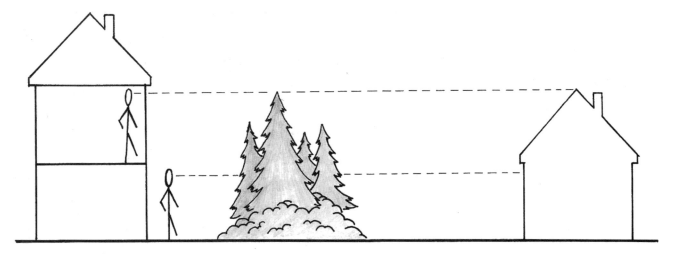

FIGURE 17: *Houses No. 2, 3, and 4 can screen every house around them—even from their second-story windows—with berms planted with evergreen trees or shrubs.*

2. A two-story house on a one-acre lot surrounded by other two-story houses on one-acre lots (Figure 17).

A twelve-foot barrier would screen views of other houses from its first-floor windows and anyplace on the grounds; an eighteen-foot barrier would screen the same views from the second-story windows.

The barriers could be any combination of berms and evergreens. The twelve-foot barrier, for example, could be a six-foot berm planted with six-foot trees or shrubs. The eighteen-foot barrier could be a ten-foot berm with eight-foot trees.

3. A two-story house on a half-acre lot (about 150 feet square), surrounded by other two-story houses, also on half-acre lots (Figure 17).

Because this house is closer to its neighbors than Nos. 1 and 2, it needs sixteen-foot barriers to screen views of other houses from its grounds and first-floor windows and twenty-two-foot barriers to screen them from its second-story windows.

To conserve space on this relatively small lot, the barriers should be relatively narrow—perhaps eight-foot berms planted with eight-foot evergreens to screen the grounds and first-

floor windows, or ten-foot berms with twelve-foot trees to screen second-story windows.

4. A two-story house on a quarter-acre lot (about one-hundred feet square) surrounded by other two-story houses on similar-size lots (Figure 17).

Because this house is even closer to its neighbors than No. 3, it needs eighteen-foot barriers to screen views from its grounds and first-floor windows and twenty-four-foot barriers to screen views from second-story windows.

Because this property has even less land than No. 3, its owner will have to build even narrower barriers. To retain a sixty-eight-foot-square space for the house, patio, play areas, etc., for example, the owner could use eight-foot berms planted with ten-foot evergreens to screen the grounds and first-floor windows, and eight-foot-berms with sixteen-foot evergreens to screen the second-story-windows. If the owner couldn't afford trees that big, he could plant smaller ones and wait for them to grow.

5. A two-story house on a relatively large urban corner lot—seventy-five feet by one-hundred—surrounded by other two-story houses on fifty-by-one-hundred-foot lots (Figure 18).

How to Create Privacy . . .

On the east side of the house is a large lawn, almost forty feet wide and more than sixty feet long. That's enough room to build a six-foot-high berm along the northern, eastern, and southern edge of the lawn and still leave enough grass for outdoor activities. Planted with ten-foot evergreen trees, the berm would be high enough to screen neighboring houses (and almost all other development) from both the lawn and the first-story windows on the east side of the house. The east side would be almost totally private, a green oasis of grass, flowers, shrubs, and trees. When the trees reached twenty-four feet high, the second story of the house would have complete privacy too.

The rest of the yard is a narrow strip of grass bordered by two streets and a service alley. As none of this space is needed for outdoor activities, it can all be given over to berms. Because the space is just fourteen to twenty feet wide, the berms can be only seven to ten feet high. But if they were planted with tall evergreen trees, they

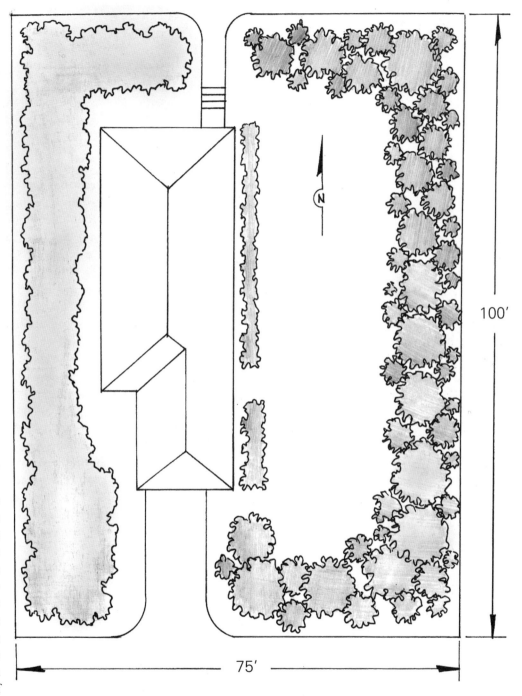

FIGURE 18: *Berms planted with evergreen trees can create substantial privacy for House No. 5—including a large, private lawn on the east side of the house.*

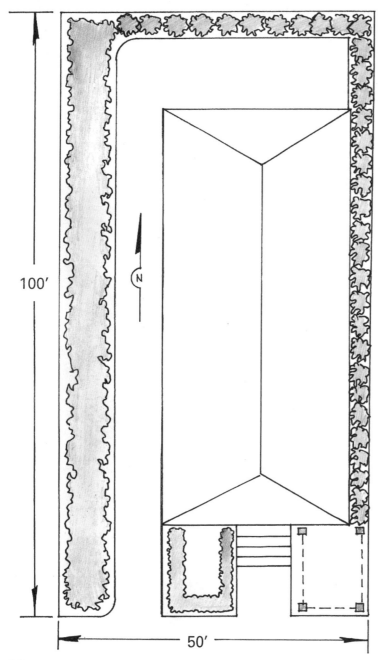

FIGURE 19: *A small berm planted with columnar evergreen trees could create a small, private outdoor room in front of House No. 6; a fence could create a slightly larger but less private space. Berms planted with evergreen trees could create privacy along the north, east, and west sides of the house.*

would immediately provide substantial privacy for the first floor of the house and, eventually, total privacy for the first floor and substantial privacy to the second. The berms would also reduce traffic and other noise and, of course, replace high-maintenance grass with low-maintenance trees and shrubs. The plantings would also create a beautiful tree-filled view from inside the house.

6. A three-story house on a fifty-by-one-hundred-foot city lot surrounded by other three-story buildings on fifty-by-one-hundred-foot lots (Figure 19)

Unlike No. 5, this house doesn't have a large lawn. It has a four-foot-wide strip of land on the east side of the house and sixteen-foot-wide strips along the north, south, and west sides. Most of the north side, however, is a paved parking area and more than half of the west side is a driveway.

The four-foot strip on the east side of the house can be filled with a tiny, two-foot-high berm, and the berm can be planted with columnar evergreen shrubs (see page 40) that will immediately screen views from first-floor rooms and soon provide screening for the second- and third-floor rooms.

Columnar evergreen trees can be planted along the northern boundary to provide screening for the north side of the house.

The eight-foot-wide strip on the western boundary, beside the driveway, already has several mature sugar maples, which provide beautiful fall color, welcome shade, and—most important—substantial screening for all three floors of the house from May to November. The trees present a difficult choice. The owner could cut them down and replace them with a four-foot berm planted with tall evergreens. That would provide year-round, not just seasonal, privacy—but only for the first floor of the house; the other floors wouldn't have privacy until the trees grew. Or he could leave the trees alone and plant evergreen shrubs beneath them. That would create substantial year-round

How to Create Privacy . . .

privacy for the first floor, but only seasonal privacy for the other floors. What to do? It depends on where the owner wants privacy and when he wants it. And on how much he loves the maples.

The south side of the house is divided into two sections by the front sidewalk, each about sixteen feet by fourteen feet. If the home is to have a private outdoor living area, this is where it has to be.

The owner could create a charming private outdoor room in one or both of these sections by building a foot-high berm along the edges of the space and planting it with a hedge of columnar evergreen shrubs. They would provide privacy for anyone inside the room and, of course, for the first floor as well. As the trees grew they'd also screen the second and third floors.

The narrow trees would absorb only a portion of the space in the room, and in any event they could be pruned if they grew too wide. If the trees took up no more than two feet on each side of the room, they would leave about fourteen by ten feet of usable area—plenty of room for a few chairs, a table, or other furniture. The room would be a fine outdoor reading, dining, or sunning area for one, two, or three people.

But what if the owner of the house wanted to be able to fit more people into the room—for outdoor entertaining and the like? In that case, he'd want to make the room as large as possible. To do that he'd have to screen not with trees, which consume several square yards of space, but with a fence, which takes up only a few inches along the sides of the room.

A fence, of course, would provide less privacy than tall trees, and it would never be tall enough to screen upper-story windows. But it would make the outdoor room more spacious, and it would be tall enough to screen it from people, passing cars, and the first floors of neighboring houses.

7. A four-story brick townhouse in a large city, built close to the street and abutting other townhouses on each side of it; its only open space is a twenty-by-twenty-four-foot back yard.

Like No. 6, this home could have a private outdoor room if the owners planted columnar evergreen shrubs around the edge of the yard. Or, if they wanted to conserve space, they could create privacy with a fence or wall.

An eight-foot board fence topped with an eight-foot lattice would screen the yard from the first and second stories of the surrounding buildings. The fence could be painted white, to match the windows of the townhouse, or dark green, to match the shutters. The owners could also build an eight-foot brick wall, which would match the exterior of the townhouse, and erect a wooden fence on top of the wall.

If the entire room were covered with a pergola, the space would be almost completely enclosed—by the rear facade of the house on one side, by fences or walls on the other sides, and by the pergola above. If the joists of the pergola were close enough together and vines on them were thick enough, views of surrounding buildings would be blocked almost completely—and almost perfect privacy would be created even in a tiny yard in the middle of a metropolis (Figure 15).

If you can't make your house perfectly private, don't despair. The goal isn't necessarily to create perfect privacy, though that's the ideal; it's to create *as much privacy as possible*. Privacy is such a good thing that every home deserves as much as it can get, and virtually every home can be made more private.

If you can't block all development around your own house, at least you can block *more* of it. If you can't be surrounded *only* by trees, shrubs, and other growing things, you *can* be surrounded by many more trees, shrubs, and other plants than you are now. If you can't create complete privacy, you can at least enjoy the satisfaction of having done everything possible to create all the privacy you can.

Once your berms, walls, fences, or pergolas are erected, it's time to plant them. That's explained in the next section.

Part 2

How to Create Large, Beautiful Gardens Economically ... with Low-Cost, Low-Maintenance Landscaping

How to Create Privacy, Color, and Interest
. . . with Low-Maintenance Trees, Shrubs, Ground Covers, and Vines

Large gardens are typically planted with room-size beds of annual and perennial flowers, many sculpted shrubs, and expanses of manicured lawn. Unfortunately, this type of gardening is the most time-consuming, labor-intensive landscaping in the world. Lawns, flowers, and groomed shrubs demand untold hours of planting, watering, weeding, fertilizing, dusting, dividing, deadheading, staking, clipping, pruning, and raking. Maintaining even an average suburban lawn, flower, and shrub garden can take twenty, thirty, or more hours a week in the summer. For some people, it's a full-time job. On estate-size properties—which have even larger lawns, bigger flower beds, and more trees and shrubs—the job requires full-time gardeners. No wonder most large high-maintenance gardens belong to the rich. (And no wonder even many of the wealthy gave them up when the Depression and the income tax lowered their vast disposable incomes, and they could no longer find skilled immigrant gardeners willing to work for a few dollars a day.)

Annuals, perennials, and deciduous shrubs have yet another drawback: For all their color and beauty, they're still just part-time plants. Perennial flowers and deciduous shrubs bloom for only a few weeks each year; worse, their foliage dies back in the fall and doesn't appear again until spring. Annuals bloom all summer, but they can't be planted until spring and they die in the fall.

If a garden consisted only of part-time plants, it would be only a part-time garden: green for just a few months and bare for as much as half the year. In cold northern climates the garden would be bare from the time herbaceous plants begin dying off in September until it snows in December or January, bare again during winter thaws, and bare from the time the snow disappears in March until perennials reemerge in May.

Happily, there are alternatives to both bare ground and high-maintenance landscaping:

- You can replace labor-intensive lawns, annual and perennial flowers, and sheared shrubbery with trees, shrubs, ground covers, and vines that largely take care of themselves.

- For year-round interest, you can cover at least half your garden—and ideally much more—with evergreens.

- You can create color not just with perennials and annuals but also with the flowers, foliage, berries, and bark of shrubs, trees, vines, and ground covers.

By planting low-maintenance trees, shrubs, and other plants, your house can be surrounded by large, lush, colorful year-round gardens. But, unlike the all-too-typical lawn-and-flower garden, your landscape will require not dozens of hours of upkeep a week, but only a few dozen hours a *year*.

Where the Plants Go

For simplicity's sake, mentally divide your property, like Caesar's Gaul, into three parts:

1. Your **house**, surrounded by shrubs and other foundation plantings, in or near the center of your lot;

2. The **Perimeter**, or boundary of your lot, where berms or other barriers may be needed to create privacy (described in Part 1);

3. The **Middle Zone**, which is the rest of your lot, the private ring of land between the Perimeter and your house, where outdoor activities take place and a terrace, a pool, a lawn, a vegetable garden, and/or other outdoor amenities can be located.

Each of these areas requires its own kinds of plants. Evergreen shrubs, for example, screen the foundation of the house; evergreen trees and shrubs provide privacy on the Perimeter; deciduous trees in the Middle Zone provide energy-saving shade for your house in the summer but allow the sun to warm your house in the winter.

This list of low-maintenance trees, shrubs, ground covers, and vines (plus a few perennials) will help you create a private, colorful, low-maintenance landscape.

When choosing plants for your yard, you first need to think, not about specific plants, but about *types* or categories of plants required for a certain effect—for example, three-foot-high evergreen shrubs to create privacy. Only after you've identified the type of plant you need can you choose the *specific* shrubs you want (Roseum Elegans rhododendrons, for instance).

My list has two paradoxes: Even though it's longer than the plant lists in many garden books, it's only a fraction of the thousands of landscape plants in existence. And even though it includes popular landscaping plants, many of them will not be available at most nurseries and garden centers. That's because the fraction of landscape plants that plant sellers have room to stock is even smaller than the fraction that I have room to list.

That, however, is not usually a problem, because what's essential in landscaping is almost never a particular plant but (again) a particular *type* or category of plant. If, for example, a nursery doesn't have the three-foot-tall Roseum Elegans rhododendrons you need for a privacy screen, it'll probably have at least one other kind of three-foot-tall catawba rhododendron that will work just as well. With plants as with people, no one is indispensable.

My list is hardly intended to be definitive. On the contrary, it's intended as a guide, a list of possibilities. Use it to compile a preliminary plant list, then see what's available at nurseries, and at what prices. You'll almost certainly find plants in every *category* you need, but probably not all of the specific plants in each category. But you will also probably find plants *not* on the list—and they might be better choices. That's partly because new cultivars, especially those of popular plants, are introduced every year. Be alert for opportunities—plants that are unusually fine, or that you especially like, or that are priced relatively low for their size. (The most popular plants are often less expensive than newer, less popular ones because they're grown in vast quantities in large wholesale nurseries.) Also look for quantity discounts, and try to find a landscape professional who'll buy plants for you wholesale.

I have space enough to describe only the highlights of each plant. If you want to know more about certain ones, you can consult references that describe them in more detail

and illustrate them with color photographs. You can also visit gardens, nurseries, and garden centers and look at the real things.

I also note the height of plants at maturity and the hardiness zones in which they grow well. The data can only be approximate because it depends on many differing factors affecting each plant, including sunlight, soil, nutrients, water, wind, humidity, etc. For most plants, I've used the hardiness zones given by Michael A. Dirr in his *Manual of Woody Landscape Plants*. Dirr's judgments tend to be more conservative than those in other references, which means (1) a plant will almost certainly do well in the zones listed and (2) it may also survive in zones that are slightly colder or warmer, if conditions are favorable. A so-called zone 4-8 plant might do fine in Zone 3, for instance, if heavy snow cover protects it in the winter. To play it safe, use the plant only in the zones given. If you don't know what zone you're in, consult the chart on page 101; if you're not sure where you fall on the chart, check with knowledgeable people in your area. To know for sure if a plant is right for your home, always ask a reliable supplier before you buy it.

Evergreen Trees for Privacy

Most evergreen trees are not as colorful as deciduous ones—they don't have dazzling spring flowers or spectacular fall foliage. They do, however, have thick year-round foliage that can provide dense, year-round screening on the Perimeter of your property. They're especially valuable on lots that need tall barriers—trees on top of berms, for instance—to create privacy. On lots that need especially high barriers, you'll need to buy tall trees or, if that's too expensive, smaller ones that grow relatively fast.

Among the fastest-growing and most versatile evergreens are **pines**. They thrive in virtually all regions of the country and in many kinds of soil.

One of the fastest-growing species is **Eastern white pine** (*Pinus strobus*). It'll grow to at least eighty feet high and forty feet wide and even bigger in especially moist climates. It will also thrive in zones 3-7, which is most of the country. Eastern white pine is known for its soft, and soft-looking, blue-green foliage. **White Mountain pine** (*P. strobus* 'White Mountain') is a vigorous cultivar with silver-blue needles.

Some people consider white pine foliage less interesting than the larger, more exotic needles that characterize most other members of the genus, including **red** or **Norway pine** (*P. resinosa*). Named for its reddish-brown bark, red pine grows a bit more slowly than Eastern white and not quite as tall. On the other hand, it can tolerate urban conditions, and it sports long, striking needles. Its range is zones 2-5.

Japanese black pine (*P. thunburgiana*) will grow quickly to as high as one-hundred feet in a cool, moist climate like the Pacific Northwest but much slower and smaller in warm, dry regions. Unlike red or Eastern white pine, this species develops a picturesque asymmetrical shape and slightly twisted trunk. Its range is zones 6-8.

Another picturesque tree is **Scotch** or **Scots pine** (*P. sylvestris*). It doesn't grow quite as fast or as big as Eastern white (it rarely tops fifty feet), but it has pretty reddish-orange bark, interesting needles and branches, and, when older, an impressive broad shape. It also has a wide range: zones 3-7.

If you live in a warmer climate, you can grow several other relatively fast-growing pines. **Knobcone pine** (*P. attenuata*) grows in zones 7-9 and can reach eighty feet. **Cluster pine** (*P. pinaster*), also known as **maritime** or **French Turpentine pine,** thrives in zones 7-10, and will reach ninety feet. **Canary Island pine** (*P. canariensis*) quickly reaches sixty to eighty feet, but it's hardy only in zones 9-10. The dense **shore pine,** or **beach pine** (*P. contorta*), grows in zones 7-10, but rarely more than thirty-five feet high. **Bishop pine** (*P. muricata*) grows in zones 8-10, but only to fifty feet and only in the West.

Other good barrier trees are **spruces** (*Picea* spp.) and **firs** (*Abies* spp.). Both generally grow slower than pines, and, unlike pines, they have a strong pyramidal or spirelike shape—so strong that they'll usually dominate any landscape in which they're planted. If you want to soften their impact, plant them in groups rather than as solitary specimens— they're excellent privacy hedges. Spruces and firs do best in a cool climate and moist soil, and their foliage remains fullest when they're grown in full sun.

Two tall, relatively fast-growing spruces are **Norway spruce** (*P. abies*) and **Sitka spruce** (*P. sitchensis*). Norway spruce grows quickly to one-hundred feet and often taller, and it has a wide range: zones 3-7. Sitka spruce will grow even faster and taller than Norway spruce, but only in zones 6-9 and in a cool, moist climate on the West Coast.

Colorado blue spruce (*P. pungens* 'Glauca') is justly celebrated for its striking steel-blue needles, and it's hardy in zones 3-7. But it grows much slower than other spruces, and never more than sixty feet tall. Use it when you don't need rapid growth to create higher screening quickly.

Among the most adaptable firs is **White fir** (*A. concolor*). It grows rather slowly to between fifty and seventy-five feet tall, it tolerates warm summers and dry weather, it grows in zones 4-7, and it has handsome bluish-green needles; the cultivar **'Violacea'** has silver-blue needles. **Grand or lowland fir** (*A. grandis*) reaches as much as one-hundred feet, but its range is only zones 6-7. **Noble fir** (*A. procera*) will grow almost as tall as grand fir, but only in the cooler and wetter higher elevations of zones 5-6 in the West. The silver-blue needles of the cultivar **'Glauca'** are as striking as those of Colorado spruce, but 'Glauca' grows even slower than the species.

Another tall evergreen is **Douglas fir** (*Pseudotsuga mensiesii*), which, from a distance, resembles a spruce. Named for its soft firlike needles, Douglas fir grows at a moderate rate, in zones 4-6. The variety **P. mensiesii glauca** has attractive bluish needles. Douglas fir can reach more than eighty feet in the East, higher in the West. It will also grow (albeit more sparsely) in shade.

The sprightly **Japanese cedar** (*Cryptomeria japonica*) is pyramidal when young, more rounded when older. It grows at a moderate rate to one-hundred feet or more and thrives in zones 6-8. It also has a picturesque red-brown bark that peels off in long strips and needles that become slightly bronze colored in cold weather.

If you live in a warm climate, you can plant **Deodar cedar** (*Cedrus deodara*). Known for its gracefully drooping branches and flopped-over top, this pyramidal evergreen grows moderately to seventy feet or more. Its range, however, is only zones 7-8. The cultivar **'Glauca'** has fine blue-gray needles. Another cultivar, **'Aurea,'** has golden-yellow needles, making it an excellent source of year-round color.

Another useful barrier tree is **Canadian** or **Eastern hemlock** (*Tsuga canadensis*). It grows only moderately and usually reaches no more than seventy feet tall. But it has three advantages: Like Douglas fir, it tolerates shade, so it can be planted where pines and spruces cannot; it grows densely, so it can usually provide more screening than other large evergreens; and its fine, soft-looking texture harmonizes easily with other plants. Canadian hemlock also has a wide range: zones 3-6. Unfortunately, at this writing the species is threatened by an infestation of woolly adelgids, insects that can kill the tree if it isn't treated with an oil spray or insecticide. If you plan to plant hemlocks soon, or if you already have some, watch for signs of the adelgid (white larvae that look like cotton batting) and be prepared to pay for treatments by professional arborists.

Western hemlock (*T. heterophylla*) grows faster and higher than Canadian hemlock, but only in zones 5-9 in the West.

All of these needle-evergreen trees won't just grow tall, of course. They'll also grow wide. Some will spread to twenty feet or more at maturity. In most yards that won't be a problem, especially if they're planted on top of berms. But on tiny urban lots or in other gardens where every square foot of space is needed for outdoor living areas, wide trees take up valuable room. In that case, your evergreen trees may need to have a narrow columnar shape.

Probably the narrowest, tallest, fastest-growing, and most adaptable columnar evergreen is **leyland cypress** (*Cupressocyparis leylandii*). This remarkable tree can grow more than three feet a year—sometimes even faster—and reaches sixty or seventy feet, so it can provide a lot of screening quickly. But even at maturity, it's never more than ten to twelve feet wide, and when younger, of course, it's much narrower; so it's a real space-saver. It also has fine, feathery blue-green foliage, it grows well in almost any conditions, and it has a wide range: zones 6-10. The cultivar **'Leighton Green'** has grayish-green foliage, **'Naylor's Blue'** has blue-green needles, and **'Castewellan'** has yellow needles.

Needle Evergreen Shrubs for Privacy

If your climate is too cold for leyland cypress, and you need narrow trees for screening, you can substitute columnar needle evergreen shrubs, such as **Hicks yew** (*Taxus media* 'Hicksii'), which grows in zones 4-7, or **arborvitae** (*Thuja* spp.) or **juniper** (*Juniperus* spp.). All these shrubs, however,

are shorter and slower growing than leyland cypress. Hicks yew, for example, grows slowly to only twenty feet. **Emerald green arborvitae** (*T. occidentalis* 'Smaragd' or 'Emerald'), named for its bright foliage, grows slowly to ten or fifteen feet—but it spreads only to three or four feet wide even at maturity, so it's another space-saver. Its zones are 3-7. **Columnar Hetz juniper** (*J. chinensis* 'Hetzii Columnaris'), which produces colorful light-green needles and dark-blue berries, reaches fifteen to twenty-five feet. The rich green **spartan juniper** (*J. chinensis* 'Spartan') quickly reaches twenty feet. Both junipers grow in zones 4-8.

A few columnar evergreens are hardy to Zone 3. The forest-green **Cologreen juniper** (*J. scoplorum* 'Cologreen'), for instance, grows fifteen to twenty feet; **Keteleer juniper** (*J. chinensis* 'Keteleeri') reaches twenty-five feet and produces grayish-green to whitish-blue fruits; the arborvitae *T. occidentalis* **'Hetz Wintergreen'** can reach thirty feet; *T. occidentalis* **'Fastigiata,'** grows to twenty-five feet.

Deciduous Trees

Unlike evergreens, deciduous trees make terrible privacy barriers, because their leaves, which do most of the screening, are on the tree only a few months of the year. In the winter, early spring, and late fall, a row of deciduous trees is only slightly more opaque than a window.

Nevertheless, these trees are invaluable because they do what evergreens don't. In the winter, their arching bare branches provide large, striking natural sculpture. Even more important is their seasonal color: Some deciduous trees produce smashing displays of seasonal blossoms. Many have colorful buds, stems, or fruits. Some provide spectacular red, orange, or yellow fall foliage. A few have red leaves all season long. And some boast two, three, or more of these features.

In other words, deciduous trees do what flowers do—but automatically and with almost no effort on your part. In fact, one of the most beneficent paradoxes in gardening is the fact that colorful deciduous trees, which require virtually no care at all, produce more color than even the most fastidiously tended flower bed. Drive around rural New England in the autumn and you'll be overwhelmed by this fact: If the meanest homestead has just one or two sugar maples, its landscape will be almost saturated with stunning orange-red foliage. For a few miraculous weeks each year it will have—thanks to nothing but the benevolence of nature—a surpassingly beautiful garden, more splendid than any other landscape I can call to mind.

And there's more: Because some deciduous trees have dense foliage, the larger species can shade, and therefore help cool, your house in warm weather, thereby making you more comfortable indoors and saving you hundreds of dollars in air-conditioning costs.

Furthermore, because deciduous trees lose their foliage in the fall, they will not shade your house in cold weather, but, on the contrary, will allow sunlight to help heat your house and thereby save you hundreds of dollars in home heating costs.

Deciduous trees also help make your property cooler by transpiring water vapor through their leaves—but only in warm weather, of course, when the trees are in leaf and the cooling is welcome.

In other words, deciduous trees are a natural thermostat. They provide free cooling in the warmest weather and allow the sun to help heat your home in the coldest months, thus helping to conserve the world's scarce oil, coal, and other fossil fuels in two different ways.

Deciduous Trees for Shade

The sun shines on your house from the east in the morning, from the south at midday, and from the west in the afternoon. To shield your home from summer sun, you should therefore plant deciduous trees on the east, south, and west sides of the house—especially the south and west, because the sun shines there in the warmest parts of the day, when shade is needed most. To create as much shade as you can, the trees should have dense foliage, and they should be large enough and tall enough to block as much of the sun's rays as possible.

Depending on how far north or south you live, the sun's rays in the summer are a sixty- to seventy-five-degree angle to the earth (see Figure 20). That means that trees tall enough to block *all* the sun's rays have to be at least several yards higher than the highest part of your house. Trees that tall, of course, are usually impossible to find in a nursery—

especially if your house is more than one story high. That's why shade trees, like evergreen trees used to create privacy on small lots, should usually be relatively fast-growing species that will reach their ideal height as quickly as possible. You can also make these trees "higher" automatically by growing them in two- or three-foot-high planting berms (see page 79).

The closer a tree is to the house, the more sun it will block (see Figure 20). Ideally, shade trees could be planted right beside the house, like foundation shrubs. Unfortunately, they have to be planted at least ten feet away from it, so their roots won't damage the foundation and their branches won't scrape your roof or siding.

As with all garden plants, choose shade trees that have not just one but several nice features, such as colorful foliage, interesting bark, or a beautiful shape. Since most fall foliage is yellow, look for trees with red or orange leaves for variety.

Among the most versatile shade trees are **maples**. They offer large size, relatively fast growth, dense foliage, and spectacular red, orange, or yellow autumn foliage. Their only liability is shallow roots—about the only things you can plant under them are small plants, such as ground covers, which have rather shallow roots themselves.

Named for both its tiny red spring flowers and brilliant scarlet autumn foliage, **red maple** (*Acer rubrum*) is dense, fast-growing (up to seventy-five feet), and hardy in zones 3-9. It's also known as a **swamp maple** because it tolerates wet areas. Its only liability (outweighed by its assets) is weak wood: its limbs sometimes break off in severe windstorms or when covered with heavy snow or ice. The variety **'October Glory'** is especially useful because its crimson foliage lingers on the tree for weeks after other maples have lost their leaves. Another variety, **'Armstrong,'** has beautiful silver-gray bark.

Hardy in zones 4-7, **Norway maple** (*A. platanoides*) also casts heavy shade and grows briskly to ninety feet or more. It's also tough, adapting easily to difficult soils and climates, even air pollution. The tree's fall foliage, however, is a rather common bright yellow. The variety **'Crimson King'** has rich maroon foliage all summer long, but it grows slowly and rarely more than forty feet tall, so it provides only a fraction of the shade of other maples. It's better used not for shade but as an ornamental tree in the Middle Zone (see page 76).

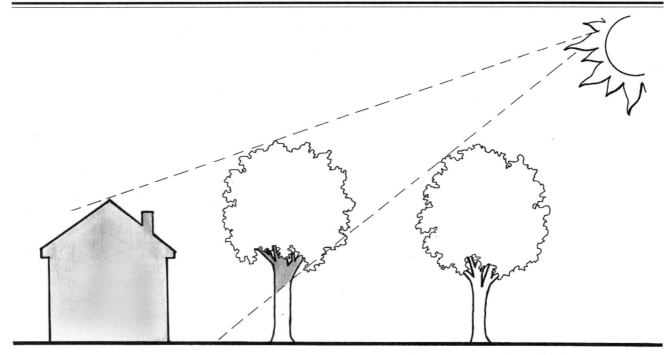

FIGURE 20: *Because the sun's rays are a sixty- to seventy-five-degree angle to the earth in the summer, trees have to be taller than your house—and relatively close to it—to shade it completely.*

Sugar maple (*A. saccharum*) doesn't grow as fast as either red or Norway maple, but it has dense foliage and, in time, can reach seventy-five feet. It also offers spectacular red, orange, or yellow fall color and an impressive shape: a short, massive trunk and short, stout branches forming an immense oval crown. Some sugar maples, such as **'Majesty'** and **'Green Mountain,'** are hardy in zones 3-7; others, including **'Bonfire'** and **'Commemoration,'** are hardy only in zones 4-7.

Several **oak** trees provide many of the benefits of maples, plus two more: Unlike maples, oaks have deep roots, so shrubs and other large plants can easily grow underneath them. Also, oak leaves tend to linger on the tree until winter, thereby providing welcome late-season color.

One of the most versatile species is the stately **red oak** (*Quercus rubra*). It grows relatively quickly to as much as eighty feet, its range is wide—zones 4-10—and it has dense foliage, which in the fall turns the rich maroon red after which the tree is named.

Hardy in zones 4-8, **pin oak** (*Q. palustris*) also grows relatively fast—to as much as seventy-five feet—and it has bronze or scarlet foliage.

The handsome spreading **white oak** (*Q. alba*), which grows in zones 4-9, can eventually grow to eighty feet high and eighty feet wide, and its fall foliage is a rich purplish red. Unfortunately, it grows very slowly.

Catalpa bean trees are esteemed less for their bright yellow fall foliage than for their immense tropical-looking, heart-shaped leaves; their two-inch-wide, trumpet-shaped white spring flowers; and their decorative ten- to twenty-inch-long seed pods that dangle from the tree after the leaves fall off, a bit like giant string beans. **Northern** or **Western Catalpa** (*Catalpa speciosa*), whose range is zones 4-8, grows rapidly to as much as sixty feet high. **Common, Eastern,** or **Southern Catalpa** (*C. bignonioides*), also known as the **Indian bean tree,** grows in zones 5-9 and reaches thirty to fifty feet. Its cultivar **'Aurea'** is named for its yellow-tinted foliage.

How to Create Privacy, Color, and Interest . . .

Beech trees also grow tall—as much as one-hundred feet—and they cast deep shade. Unfortunately, they grow slowly, so when they're young they'll shade only the lower part of your house. Beeches, however, may be worth waiting for because of their attractive smooth gray bark; their golden brown autumn leaves, which (like oak leaves) linger well into the winter; their handsome gnarled, bulging trunks (when the tree is older); their stately low-hanging branches; and, most of all, the beautiful colored foliage of several cultivars of **European beech** (*Fagus sylvatica*). Perhaps the best colored-leaf beech is *F. sylvatica* 'Riversii' (sometimes sold as 'Atropunicea' or 'Purpurea'). Unlike other purple beeches, 'Riversii' retains its deep purple or red purple leaf color all summer long. Like other European birches, it grows in zones 4-7.

If you live in a relatively mild climate (Zone 6 or warmer), you can also shade your house with one of the larger types of dogwood, described in the next section.

Deciduous Trees for Color

Many deciduous trees are too short, too slow-growing, or too lightly leafed to be good shade trees. But what these little trees lack in size they make up for in the showy colors of their flowers, foliage, berries, or bark. Like perennial flowers, they automatically create great masses of color, year after year, that are actually more impressive than many flower borders. What's more, this color will be in the branches and/or trunks of the trees; it won't be confined to the ground, like flowers, but will rise up the walls and even to the ceilings of outdoor rooms.

To get as much as you can out of these ornamental trees, choose species that give you color in more than one season—not only spring or summer flowers, but also colorful fall foliage and winter berries. And don't plant only spring bloomers. Extend your color season by adding trees that flower in summer and early fall.

In a perfect world, the trees in our garden would somehow be colorful all year. They're not, of course; on the contrary, for most of the year, in most of the country, deciduous trees are either covered with nothing but green leaves or they're completely bare. But if we can't have trees with year-round color, we *can* have trees that give us the most color possible, as often as possible.

Among the most colorful ornamentals are **Japanese maples** (*A. palmatum*). Many cultivars of this small, broad, slow-growing tree, which is hardy in zones 5-8, provide impressive shades of red or maroon foliage from midspring to midfall. 'Bloodgood' and 'Crimson Prince,' for instance, have deep-red leaves; 'Red Dragon' has dark, purple-maroon foliage. The scarlet leaves of 'Shindeshojo' are dazzling in the spring.

Many Japanese maples display their summer-long color on delicate, deeply lobed or dissected leaves. 'Crimson Queen,' for instance, has bright crimson-red summer foliage that turns scarlet in autumn. 'Ever-Red' has deep purple-red leaves. 'Garnet' is named for the rich color of its summer foliage, which turns a lighter red in the fall. The larger leaves of 'Inaba Shidare' are red-maroon in the summer and crimson in the fall. The foliage of 'Tamukeyama' is crimson at first, then purple-red, then bright scarlet in autumn.

Among the most colorful flowering ornamental trees are **dogwoods** (see photograph, page 52). These graceful plants produce beautiful white, pink, or red blossoms (actually bracts) for several weeks in the spring—twice as long as many other flowering trees. Dogwoods also offer brilliant red fall foliage, colorful berrylike fruits (beloved by birds), and a handsome winter silhouette; some varieties have pretty variegated foliage. Unlike most other flowering trees, dogwoods will tolerate (even welcome) a little shade.

In the spring, **flowering dogwood** (*Cornus florida*) is covered with large white bracts, some as much as four inches across. In the fall, it's covered with deep-red leaves and glossy red berries, which stay on the tree until they're eaten by birds. Flowering dogwood also has a wide range—zones 5-9.

The varieties 'Apple Blossom' and 'Spring Song' have pink bracts. **Pink flowering dogwood** (*C. florida rubra*) has reddish pink bracts. **Cherokee chief red dogwood** (*C. florida* 'Cherokee Chief') has rosy red ones. 'Cherokee Princess,' 'Cloud 9,' and 'White Cloud' are known for their especially large profusion of relatively large white bracts. As its name suggests, 'Fragrant White Cloud' is sweet-scented. The variegated leaves of 'Welchii' are creamy white, pink, deep rose, and green (though its flowers are not as conspicuous). **'Rainbow'** has variegated yellow-and-green leaves. **'Cherokee Daybreak'** has variegated white-and-green foliage.

Like flowering dogwood, **Kousa** or **Japanese dogwood** (*C. kousa*) has white bracts and red fall foliage. But it also has big red autumn fruits that look like strawberries, and it blooms in early summer, several weeks after the flowering dogwood. It's also more resistant than flowering dogwood to deadly dogwood borers and anthracnose, a fungal disease. **Chinese dogwood** (*C. kousa chinensis*) has slightly larger bracts than Japanese dogwood. Both trees grow in zones 5-8.

If you live in zones 5-7, you can grow—and shade your house with—**giant dogwood** (*C. controversa*). This handsome tree has an elegant pyramidal crown and grows quickly to between thirty and forty-five feet. In spring, before foliage appears, the tree is blanketed with huge clusters of creamy white flowers. In late summer, half-inch-wide blue-black fruits appear, followed by bright-red foliage in the fall.

If you live in zones 7-9 in the West, you can grow **Pacific** or **Western dogwood** (*C. nuttallii*), the biggest dogwood of all. This tree will grow to fifty feet or more, and it produces some of the largest blossoms of the genus. Its white bracts appear not only in spring but often in late summer as well. The tree also offers yellow or red foliage and dense clusters of orange-red berries in the fall. The variety **'Goldspot'** has variegated green-and-creamy-yellow leaves and bracts that are even larger than the species.'

Flowering fruit trees (crabapples, plums, cherries, pears, etc.) are also known for showy displays of white, pink, or red flowers in spring and colorful late-season fruits. Unlike dogwoods, however, fruit trees bloom for only a couple of weeks, and only a few varieties have colorful foliage. For much of the year, they're just another small deciduous tree. So use them sparingly and, to get the most out of them, choose varieties with colorful summer and/or fall foliage. These are some good choices:

Adams crabapple (*Malus* 'Adams') has red flower buds, pink flowers, carmine-red three-quarter-inch fruits and orange-red fall foliage. **Brandywine crabapple** (*M.* 'Brandywine') produces large, fragrant deep-rose double flowers, light-green fruits, yellow-green summer foliage, and deep-purple fall foliage. **Royalty crabapple** (*M.* 'Royalty')

has (sparse) crimson flowers, deep-red fruits, glossy purple leaves in spring, purple-green summer foliage, and brilliant purple leaves in the fall. **Thunderchild crabapple** (*M.* 'Thunderchild') has rose-colored flowers, dark-red or purple fruits, and deep-purple summer foliage. **Zumi** or **redbud crabapple** (*M. zumi* 'Calocarpa') produces red buds, profuse fragrant white flowers, bright-red fruits loved by birds, and orange or yellow fall foliage. All these varieties grow in zones 4-8. **Coralburst crabapple** (*M.* 'Coralburst') has coral-pink buds, profuse double rose-pink flowers, and golden-yellow fall foliage. Its range is zones 3-7.

Newport flowering plum (*Prunus cerasifera* 'Newport') has pale-pink flowers, inch-thick dull purple fruits, and dark-purple summer foliage. **Mt. St. Helen's plum** (*P. cerasifera* 'Mt. St. Helen') has an even richer purple leaf color than 'Newport.' **Thundercloud plum** (*P. cerasifera* 'Thundercloud') produces fragrant pink flowers and deep-purple summer foliage. All three trees grow in zones 5-8.

Mist cherry (*P.* 'Hally Jolivette') is named for the "mist" effect created by its mass of tiny double white flowers that bloom for two to three weeks. The tree, which grows in zones 5-7, also has red fall foliage and a smooth mahogany-colored bark that exfoliates in curly paper-thin sheets.

Kwanzan cherry (*P. serrulata* 'Kwanzan') produces two-and-one-half-inch-wide double pink flowers and orange-bronze fall foliage. **Accolade flowering cherry** (*P. subhirtella* 'Accolade') has semidouble pink flowers and bright-orange fall foliage. The well-named **weeping snow fountains cherry** (*P. subhirtella* 'Pendula x Snow Fountains') has snowy semidouble flowers on graceful branches that reach the ground, creating a fountainlike effect. The tree also has beautiful orange-and-gold fall foliage. **Autumn-flowering cherry** (*P. subhirtella* 'Autumnalis') is an especially useful variety because it produces pink buds in summer, pink flowers in a *mild* autumn, and still more flowers in the spring. All four cultivars grow in zones 5-8.

Hardy in zones 4-7, the beautiful **sargent cherry** (*P. sargentii*) has pink flowers; shiny chestnut-colored or reddish-brown bark; and foliage that's reddish tinged when new, shiny dark green in the summer, and yellow, orange, or red in the fall.

Canada red cherry (*P. virginiana* 'Schubert') has white flowers and impressive deep maroon summer foliage. Unlike most cherries, its range is zones 2-6.

Hardy in zones 5-8, **flowering pear** (*Pyrus calleryana*) offers white flowers and very colorful fall foliage. One of the best, **Bradford flowering pear** (*P. calleryana* 'Bradford'), has profuse white flowers and handsome thick green leaves that turn red or deep crimson in the fall. **Aristocrat flowering pear** (*P. calleryana* 'Aristocrat') produces clustered white flowers and brilliant purple-red fall foliage.

The many cultivars of **serviceberry** (*Amelanchier arborea*), also known as **shadbush** or **shadblow,** produce white or pink spring flowers; red, purple, or black fruits (some of them edible); and bright yellow, orange, or red fall foliage. Hardy in zones 4-8, serviceberries also tolerate partial shade.

The new foliage of the elegant **Katsura tree** (*Cercidiphyllum japonicum*) creates a red-purple "haze" in springtime; in the autumn the leaves turn a bright yellow or red. Katsura trees grow in zones 4-8.

The graceful **redbud** is covered with reddish, white, or purple flowers in spring and yellow foliage in the fall. **Eastern redbud** (*Cercis canadensis*) has reddish-purple flowers, **white redbud** (*C. canadensis alba*) has pure white flowers, and **'Oklahoma'** has wine red blossoms; all grow in zones 4-8. **Forest Pansy redbud** (*C. canadensis* 'Forest Pansy') produces both rose-purple flowers and striking red-purple foliage (which later becomes more subdued) in the spring. Its range is zones 6-8.

Fringetrees sport thick clusters of tiny, fragrant white flowers in late spring and bright yellow foliage in the fall. **Chinese fringetree** (*Chionanthus retusus*), which grows in zones 6-8, also has lustrous leathery leaves and handsome exfoliating gray-brown bark. **White fringetree** (*C. virginicus*), which grows in zones 4-9, produces fragrant flowers in May and June—later than Chinese fringetrees—and then clusters of blue grapelike fruit.

To bring color into your yard not just in springtime but throughout the year, you'll also need to plant trees that bloom in the summer, fall, and winter.

Goldenchain tree (*Laburnum watereri*) doesn't have colorful fruit or foliage, and it's poisonous if eaten. But it does create spectacular displays of fragrant yellow wisterialike flowers, in chainlike clusters as much as twenty inches long, in May or June. Its range is zones 5-7.

Hardy in zones 5-8, **Japanese snowbell** or **Japanese snowdrop** tree (*Styrax japonica*) produces pendulous clusters of white bell-shaped flowers in late spring, showy grayish fruit in late summer, and yellow or reddish foliage in the fall. **Fragrant snowbell** (*S. obassia*) is named for its sweet-scented flowers. Both trees grow in zones 7-9.

Japanese tree lilac (*Syringa reticulata*) doesn't have colorful foliage, but it does produce very fragrant, very showy clusters of white flowers in June. It also has a wide range—zones 3-7—and sports attractive reddish-brown bark.

The handsome **Stewartias** are known for white camellialike flowers that bloom for several weeks in July, as well as for deep-green leaves, colorful autumn foliage, and attractive peeling bark. **Korean stewartia** (*Stewartia koreana*) has three-inch-wide flowers with a prominent cluster of orange-yellow stamens in the center. Its dark-brown bark flakes to reveal green patches underneath, and its fall foliage is a bright orange, red, or reddish purple. The somewhat taller **Japanese stewartia** (*S. pseudocamellia*) has slightly smaller flowers and showy orange anthers; yellow, red, or reddish purple fall foliage; and exfoliating red-brown bark. Both trees grow in zones 5-7.

Sourwood (*Oxydendrum arboreum*) is also called the **lily-of-the-valley tree** because of the long fingers of tiny white bell-shaped flowers that cover the tree in midsummer. Sourwood, which grows in zones 5-9, also has attractive gray bark and lustrous green leaves that turn a brilliant scarlet or purple-red in the fall.

Goldenraintree (*Koelreuteria paniculata*) is also a tree of many colors: Its foliage is purplish-red at first, then red, then bright-green, then golden-yellow in the fall; its midsummer flowers are a striking yellow; and its seedpods, which look like tiny Japanese lanterns, are red when new, buff-colored when older. Goldenraintree grows in zones 5-8. **September goldenraintree** (*K. paniculata* 'September') is especially valuable because it's one of only a few trees that flowers in (as its name suggests) September. The related **Chinese flame tree** (*K. henryi*) is similar to the goldenraintree, except that its seedpods are red, orange, or salmon, and it grows only in zones 9-10.

Franklinia (*Franklinia alatamaha*) is another very useful tree because its fragrant, striking three-inch-wide camellialike flowers appear in August and September, when most other plants have already flowered. Franklinia also produces red or orange fall foliage. Its range is zones 5-8.

Witchhazel is valuable because it's the only tree that blooms in the winter in cold climates. Probably the showiest witchhazels are the ***Hamamelis*** x ***intermedia*** cultivars, whose range is zones 5-8. One of the best is **'Arnold promise,'** which sports large, fragrant yellow flowers in late winter and yellow, orange, or red foliage in the fall.

If you live in milder climates, you can plant even more varieties of late-flowering trees. In zones 7-9 you can grow **Crape myrtle** (*Lagerstroemia indica*), which has spectacular dense clusters of red, rose, pink, lavender, purple, or white flowers in late summer. Crape myrtle also has red, orange, or yellow fall foliage and smooth grayish-brown bark that peels off to reveal multicolored pinkish, brown, or gray bark underneath.

If you live in zones 8-10 you can grow **Natal Coral Tree** (*Erythrina humeana*), which has bright orange flowers from late summer through most of the fall.

Other deciduous trees create their most striking color not with their flowers or foliage but with their bark. Ideally, every garden would have at least one cluster of white birches, whose trunks provide large swatches of white all year long. **Canoe** or **paper birch** (*Betula papyrifera*) is named for its chalk-white, paperlike bark that American Indians once used to build canoes. The bark peels to reveal reddish-orange bark underneath. Canoe birch grows fifty to seventy feet—it's one of the tallest birches—and it has a wide range: zones 2-6. **Himalayan birch** (*B. jacquemontii*), which grows in zones 5-6, has pure white bark that extends even to the tips of its twigs. **Japanese whitespire birch** (*B. platyphylla* 'Whitespire') also has pure white bark, as well as glossy green foliage. It grows in zones 5-6, and is especially resistant to the bronze birch borer, a small grub that preys on birches and can easily kill, or at least maim, any tree it attacks. The vivid purple leaves of **purple rain birch** (*B. pendula* 'Purple Rain') contrast beautifully with its white bark. This well-named tree is also very hardy—its range is zones 2-6—but, like all European birches, it's more susceptible than other members of the genus to the bronze birch borer.

Broadleaf Evergreen Shrubs

Evergreen shrubs are valuable—sometimes indispensable—in two sections of your yard.

◕ They're indispensable beside your house because only evergreen plants, with their year-round foliage, can hide its foundation, provide a visual base, and soften its lines year round (see pages 75-76).

◕ They're valuable along the Perimeter of larger lots because, on bigger properties, privacy can be created by evergreen shrubs instead of larger, more expensive evergreen trees (see pages 74-75).

Not all evergreen shrubs, however, are created equal. *Broadleaf* evergreens, such as rhododendrons, azaleas, and other ericaceous plants, are more useful than *needle* evergreens, such as yews or junipers. While any evergreen shrub can provide year-round screening, only broadleaf evergreens produce beautiful spring or summer flowers. Many broadleaf evergreen shrubs have yet another bonus: They tolerate, even prefer, light or partial shade, so they do just fine in both sunny and slightly shady areas.

To get the most out of broadleaf evergreens, pick plants with the most colorful features—including variegated foliage—and choose a combination that will give you the longest period of bloom.

More than a dozen genera of handsome broadleaf evergreen shrubs are hardy in cold winter climates (which include most of the country), but the most popular, justifiably, is **Rhododendron.** Many rhododendrons are distinguished by their unusually long, smooth, leathery, dark-green oval leaves—among the largest of any shrub. Rhodies also have some of the largest flower clusters of any broadleaf evergreen—tight, rounded groups known as trusses that are ten inches wide in some species—as well as the most flower colors: many different shades of white, red, pink, purple, lavender, and mauve, as well as yellow and orange. Both their foliage and their flowers give rhododendrons a matchless presence.

Most rhododendrons bloom in May. But several small-leaf cultivars bloom as early as late April, before most other broadleaf shrubs. The justly celebrated **P. J. M.** (*Rhododendron* 'P. J. M.'), for example, sports masses of lavender-pink flowers in late April (as well as striking dark mahogany leaves in the winter). (See photographs, pages 51-52.) **White P. J. M.** (*R.* 'P. J. M. White'), as its name implies, has white flowers. Both shrubs are hardy in zones 4-8 and, unlike other rhodies, they prefer full sun.

Another early bloomer is **'April Snow,'** named for its double white flowers that appear in late April; it also has distinctive yellow stems. Blooming only slightly later are the compact, slow-growing **'Balta,'** which has pale pink, almost white flowers; **'Black Satin,'** which has large, purple-violet flowers, plus mahogany-black foliage in spring, fall, and winter; the low, wide-spreading **'Purple Gem,'** which has purple-blue flowers and bronze leaves in winter; and **'Olga Mezitt,'** which produces profuse pink blossoms and bronzy copper winter foliage. All are hardy in zones 4-8 and, like P. J. M. rhododendrons, they flower best in full sun.

Two rhodies that bloom in late April and early May are **Cunningham's white** (*R. catawbiense* 'Cunningham'), which has white flowers and is hardy in zones 5-8, and the compact **Cloudland** (*R. impeditum*), which has small bluish-purple flowers and is hardy in zones 5-6.

The tall, large-leafed Catawba cultivars bloom in mid- to late spring and can grow six to ten feet tall. **Roseum Elegans** (*R. catawbiense* 'Roseum Elegans') produces lavender-pink flowers (see photograph, page 49). **White Catawba** (*R. catawbiense* 'Album') has white flowers; **Elegans Catawba** (*R. catawbiense* 'Album Elegans') has blush-colored blossoms; **English Roseum** (*R. catawbiense* 'English Roseum') has pink flowers; **Everest** (*R. catawbiense* 'Everestianum') has rosy lilac flowers with frilly edges; and **Nova Zembla** (*R. catawbiense* 'Nova Zembla') has dark red flowers. They're all hardy in zones 4-8.

Rosebay rhododendrons (*R. maximum*) produce white, purplish-pink, or rose-colored flowers as late as early August. Several cultivars have reliably pink flowers. Rosebays are special in several ways: They're one of the few rhododendrons hardy in zones 3-7. Unlike other rhodies, they bloom in deep shade. And they're one of the largest species in the genus: They can grow to more than twenty feet tall and at least as wide. Needless to say, they're ideal for privacy barriers, shady spots, and very cold temperatures (see photograph, page 53).

Most rhododendrons can't grow in hot climates, but a few tropical species—such as **R. zolleri**—will adapt to Zone 10 and other frost-free areas.

Azaleas, which are actually rhododendrons, are grouped under their own name because they have many things in common. They're typically smaller than other rhododendrons, with smaller flower clusters and smaller leaves. They also tolerate warmer and drier conditions than rhododendrons do, and with enough sunlight they can create even more spectacular color. In the spring they're often totally covered with blossoms—a feat seldom matched by any other shrub (see photographs, pages 56-57). Some varieties also have colorful fall and/or winter foliage. **'Delaware Valley White,'** for example, has white flowers and bright yellow fall foliage. **'Hino Crimson'** has brilliant red blossoms and dark red fall foliage. **'Mother's Day'** produces large red flowers and reddish winter foliage. **'Stewartstonian'** has bright red blossoms and wine-red winter leaves. All four plants grow in zones 6-8 and they bloom in mid-spring.

(There are even more *deciduous* azaleas than evergreen ones. See page 64.)

Mountain laurel (*Kalmia latifolia*) is celebrated for its large clusters of exquisite five-sided, cup-shaped white flowers that appear in late spring. More than two dozen cultivars have showy pink blossoms. Mountain laurels are large shrubs—they can reach eight feet high in northern states—but they tend to grow open and leggy as they age, so they don't make as good a privacy screen as rhododendrons do. Most varieties grow in zones 4-8.

Sheep laurel (*K. angustifolia*), also known as **lambkill** because it's poisonous to sheep, is a low-growing shrub that likes moisture. It's valuable because it's hardy in zones 1-6 and it blooms in June or July—later than most shrubs. Its rich lavender-rose flowers resemble mountain laurel's in shape, and its several cultivars have white or pink blossoms. Like mountain laurel, it flowers best in full sun.

Japanese andromeda (*Pieris japonica*) is known for its showy pendulous clusters of white lily-of-the-valley-like flowers in early to midspring and its unique shiny, pointed, dark green wavy leaves. Its new foliage is scarlet.

Hardy in zones 5-7, Japanese andromeda has several excellent cultivars. **Crisp-leaf andromeda** (*P. japonica* 'Crispa') has wavy-margined leaves. **'Mountain Fire'** and **'Forest Flame'** have fire-red new foliage, and 'Mountain Fire' has another bonus—it blooms early, in March and April. Several varieties, including **'Dorothy Wycoff,'** **'Flamingo,'** **'Valley Rose,'** and **'Wada,'** have pink flowers. In winter 'Dorothy Wycoff' also has deep pink buds and wine-red foliage.

Hardy in zones 4-6, **mountain andromeda** (*P. floribunda*) has prominent pale white buds in winter and early spring and upright (not pendulous) clusters of fragrant white blossoms in midspring (photograph, page 52). Its foliage, however, is not as interesting or as colorful as Japanese andromeda's.

A hybrid of mountain and Japanese andromeda, the dense, wide-spreading **Brouwer's Beauty** (*P.* 'Brouwer's Beauty') has showy deep-purplish-red buds in winter and early spring. Its range is zones 5-7.

Chinese andromeda (*P. forrestii*) is taller than either Japanese or mountain andromeda—it reaches ten feet or more—and it has longer leaves, but it's hardy only in zones 7-8.

Like andromeda, *leucothoe* produces clusters of tiny white spring flowers that resemble lily-of-the-valley, and its foliage changes color with the seasons. Unlike most broadleaf evergreens, however, leucothoe is wide spreading and low-growing—seldom more than two or three feet high—and its foliage is usually more impressive than its flowers. In the spring **Girard's Rainbow** (*Leucothoe fontanesiana* 'Girard's Rainbow') produces a "rainbow" of variegated yellow, green, and pink leaves that later turn variegated green and white. **Nana** (*L. fontanesiana* 'Nana') is a dwarf variety that also has variegated white-and-green leaves. The foliage of **Scarletta** (*L. fontanesiana* 'Scarletta') is a rich scarlet in spring, dark green in summer, and different shades of burgundy in winter. **Compact drooping leucothoe** (*L. fontanesiana* 'Compacta') has bright burgundy winter foliage and fragrant flowers, and it's hardy in zones 4-8. All the other types grow in zones 5-8.

Coast leucothoe (*L. axillaris*) is even lower and wider spreading than the drooping types (*L. fontanesiana*). It has bronze to purplish winter foliage—not as colorful as drooping leucothoe's—and it's hardy in zones 5-8.

Unlike other evergreen shrubs, leucothoe's random arching branches sometimes look messy. For best effect, plant it close together in masses and trim off its longer shoots if they displease you.

Two of the most valuable shrubs in almost any garden are the white-variegated **Emerald Gaiety euonymus** (*Euonymus fortunei* 'Emerald Gaiety'), also known as Emerald Gaiety wintercreeper (photograph, page 49), and the yellow-variegated **Emerald 'n Gold euonymus** (*E. fortunei* 'Emerald 'n Gold'), also known as Emerald 'n Gold wintercreeper (photograph, page 53). Hardy in zones 5-8, these shrubs are welcome for three reasons: They provide year-round white or gold color, they flourish even in deep shade, and they climb, vinelike, up rocks and trees (and unlike some other vines, they don't harm the tree). If they have nothing to climb, they spread, typically growing five or six feet wide and never more than two or three feet high. New variegated-leaf varieties are introduced regularly; if any have more yellow or white leaf color than Emerald Gaiety or Emerald 'n Gold, consider using them instead. **Sarcoxie wintercreeper** (*E. fortunei* 'Sarcoxie') and other green-leaf types are much less useful, simply because they're not variegated.

Another interesting shrub is **Oregon grape** (*Mahonia aquifolium*). Its lustrous, dark-green hollylike leaves are pointed and slightly prickly on the edges; they're reddish bronze when new and purplish bronze in fall and winter. Oregon grape also has showy bright-yellow flowers that turn into grapelike clusters of blue-black berries that taste a bit like currants. It grows between three and five feet tall and is hardy in zones 5-7.

If you live in or south of Zone 6 (which includes all of the South, the lower Midwest, and much of the Mid-Atlantic region), you can grow two evergreen shrubs renowned for their fall and winter berries.

In addition to lustrous dark-green foliage and clusters of tiny white spring flowers, **firethorn** (*Pyracantha*) bears large,

(continued on page 61)

1 *A large berm planted with Roseum Elegans rhododendrons helps screen the entrance to Evergreen from development around it. The berm blocks the street on the far side of the berm and conceals all the houses nearby.*

Most of the plants are shrubs or ground covers that require very little care. The lavender-pink blossoms of the rhododendrons create a huge swatch of color in late spring, and the shrub's long, leathery evergreen leaves are striking year round. At the edge of the driveway, the evergreen foliage of Emerald Gaiety euonymus provides green and white color all year long. The rhododendrons are especially dramatic because they're planted in a large sweep, and the berm is a terrific platform to display them.

The purple-leaf sand cherry, at left, and the red-leaved Japanese barberry provide large spotches of striking foliage color from spring to fall.

2 *When you look toward the sculpture of the Virgin Mary and the rhododendrons behind it, you are also looking directly toward the street in front of Evergreen. You can't see any houses, however, because the view is blocked by the rhododendrons and the ten-foot-high berm on which they're planted. Instead of development, you see only the lush, low-maintenance plantings of a woodland garden.*

The evergreen ground cover around the sculpture is vinca minor, and the red accents are impatiens, annuals that flower even in deep shade.

The pool is made of black fiberglass, which is hidden by the large, flat, carefully placed fieldstones around it.

3 *Like most properties in Manchester, New Hampshire, Chris and Bill Windler's lot is small—just 100 feet by 114—and most of it was once exposed to a wide, busy street. To create a secluded spot for a patio, they built a four- to five-foot-high berm along the south and east sides of their corner lot and planted it mostly with low-maintenance evergreen shrubs. P. J. M. rhododendrons along the top of the berm create stunning lavender-pink color in early spring. All the shrubs and ground covers are arranged in large sweeps. Supported by the berm, they make a sumptuous mass of verdure that puts the plain lawns of the neighboring houses to shame. Design by Mark Rynearson.*

4 *The Windlers' berm (Photograph 3) creates a wonderful leafy enclosure for their patio. Spring color is produced by the pink-tinted white bracts of the dogwood trees and the white flowers of mountain andromeda, both of which beautifully offset the massed rose-pink flowers of the P. J. M. rhododendrons. Still more color comes from the variegated white-and-green leaves of hostas. Carpets of evergreen ground covers—wintercreeper and pachysandra—create year-round interest with their deep-green foliage.*

The handsome granite blocks form raised planting beds and provide low-maintenance seating. The brick floor of the patio is laid in a pleasing herringbone pattern. Unlike, say, wooden benches and a wooden deck, the granite benches and the brick patio will last indefinitely with virtually no care. Design by Mark Rynearson.

5 *Like almost everything else in Evergreen, our patio is a low-maintenance amenity. Its gray slate stones are laid around, and harmonize with, the gray granite rocks that were already on the site. The patio is enclosed by a low berm planted with evergreen shrubs—rosebay rhododendrons and Emerald 'n Gold euonymus—and vinca minor. Variegated white-and-green-leaf hostas provide summer-long color accents, as do the fuscia flowers of impatiens. The gray flower pots harmonize with the gray stones, and the easy repetition of the same flower color gives the composition the strength of simplicity.*

6 When the stone wall that once stood in this spot began to fall over, I had to replace it. The old wall was so high that the ground on top of it was nearly level. The new wall is less than half as tall as the old one—high enough to stop the earth from falling into the driveway, but low enough to create a steep slope on top of it. The slope, however, is not a liability but an asset. Like a berm, it's an excellent platform to display plants, including a Mugo pine, red impatiens, and sweeps of vinca minor and ground phlox, which creates impressive sheets of white and lavender blossoms in springtime. Also, the new, low wall cost less than half as much as rebuilding the old, high one would have cost. If I had re-created the old wall, it would have been another example of an expensive and unnecessary retaining wall (see pages 92-94).

7   *This sweep of hosta at Evergreen is a stunning composition for four reasons: First, it's massive—about twenty feet by sixteen. Second, it's planted on a slope for even more emphasis. Third, it's simple—it consists of just one type of plant: variegated green-and-white hostas. Fourth, it's a tapestry of foliage that becomes increasingly white toward its center. Most of the plants on the edges of the sweep are* Hosta undulata *'Albomarginata,' whose leaves have only a little bit of white, on the margins. Closer to the middle are* Hosta undulata *'Mediovariegata,' whose leaves have large white splotches in their centers. In the center of the sweep are 'Mediovariegata' plants with the very whitest leaves. This gradual whitening of the sweep creates welcome variety while allowing unity at the same time.*

    Many plant grouping have too much variety and not enough unity. The balance—which should always tip toward unity—is hard to achieve. When in doubt, simplify (see page 78).

8   *In the Spring Garden at Airlie in Wilmington, North Carolina, more than an acre is covered almost entirely with azaleas—gorgeous proof that a beautiful, colorful garden can be composed exclusively of low-maintenance shrubs. Indeed, the simplicity of the planting—just one kind of plant, arranged in large sweeps of just one color—is precisely what makes it so powerful.   The glistening classical statue of the water-bearing woman is a lively, low-maintenance year-round focal point.*

9 *This composition at the edge of the Spring Garden at Airlie (Photograph 8) shows how a beautiful landscape can consist solely of low-maintenance trees, shrubs, and ground covers. The leisurely mood of the composition is set by the sprawling limbs of a massive live oak (*Quercus virginiana*), which are both natural sculpture and a platform for ivy, which cascades down the branches and forms a thick carpet on the garden floor. The heavy limbs are a wonderful contrast to the delicate blossoms of the azaleas, and the brilliant pink and white flowers are dramatically offset by the deep, dark foliage of the ivy. This vignette needs virtually no care; it grows beautifully almost all by itself.*

10 *Much of the Descanso Garden, near Los Angeles, is composed of impressive tree-shrub-and-ground-cover arrangements like this one. Large pink and white camellias grow beneath picturesquely twisting branches of California live oaks (Quercus agrifolia), and the forest floor is carpeted with ivy. All these plants are evergreen, so the garden is appealing even when the camellias are not blooming. Also, this is a nearly self-sustaining planting, because oak leaves decay slowly, creating a deep mulch that fertilizes the plants, retains moisture, and helps keep the garden virtually weed free. (Photograph by Descanso Gardens.)*

11   *The picturesque granite cliffs at Evergreen contrast vividly with the sweep of jewelweed* (Impatiens capensis) *below them. The cliffs are rough, hard, and heavy, the essence of permanence, while the jewelweed is a light, soft perennial, delicate and fleeting. Both the cliffs and the jewelweed were the result of gardening by subtraction (see pages 87-88). The cliffs, of course, were already on the site. Much of them, however, had been buried under the remains of pine trees that had been cut a few years earlier. When the slash was removed, the cliffs were fully exposed, and there was nothing left to clutter up the view. Then, miraculously, a pure, unbroken sweep of jewelweed appeared where the pine slash was.*

*   The cliffs and the plants, in other words, were generous gifts of nature. All I had to do was unwrap the rock and give the jewelweed room to grow. Gardening by subtraction is rarely better than this.*

12 The brook at Evergreen splatters on moss-covered granite rocks. Like the handsome cliffs described in Photo 11, the stream is another example of how a garden can be made of natural features already on the site (page 88). The brook and its impressive mossy bed were a part of Evergreen when I bought the property, but they were all but hidden by thick growths of scraggly honeysuckles and woody debris. When, however, I subtracted the shrubs and the debris—voila!—there, underneath, was the brook, burbling and cascading prettily over its rock bed. The stream was another gift of nature, which, like the cliffs, I had only to unwrap.

dense, dazzling clusters of red or orange berries that create splotches of color all winter long. **Scarlet firethorn** (*P. coccinea*) has bright-red berries and grows in zones 6-9. The cultivar **'Lalandei'** (*P. coccinea* 'Lalandei') has orange-red berries. Other firethorns have larger flowers and fruit, but they do well only in zones 7-9.

Besides their long-lasting berries, **cotoneasters** are known for their dark-green leaves, white or pink spring flowers, and especially their wonderful intriguing displays of long, arching branches. **Bearberry cotoneaster** (*C. dammeri* 'Skogsholm') is a low shrub that resembles its namesake, *Arctostaphylos uva-ursi* (see page 68). It's rarely more than eighteen inches tall, and it looks great in rock gardens and draping over walls. **Willowleaf cotoneaster** (*C. salicifolius*) grows from seven to twelve feet tall, and its leaves often have reddish veins. **Parney cotoneaster** (*C. lacteus*) can grow to twelve feet tall. All three shrubs have white flowers and red berries. **Rockspray cotoneaster** (*C. horizontalis*) is another low-spreading variety, with pink flowers and red berries and red or purple fall foliage. The dense **cranberry cotoneaster** (*C. apiculatus*) has pink flowers and scarlet berries and grows to three feet high. Most cotoneasters are hardy in zones colder than 6, but I've listed them in this section because they are reliably *evergreen* only in Zone 6 or in zones warmer than 6. All the plants listed will grow well as far south as Zone 7—except parney cotoneaster, whose range is zones 7-8.

Evergreen in zones 6-9 is **lavender cotton** (*Santolina chamaecyparissus*), a low, one- to two-foot-high shrub distinguished by its silver-gray foliage and bright yellow three-quarter-inch-wide flowers that bloom in the summer.

If you live in zones 7-9 (most of which is in the South or Far West), your selection of evergreen shrubs is even larger.

Daphne is a slow-growing plant known for its clusters of very pretty small, fragrant spring flowers. **Fragrant**, or **winter daphne** (*Daphne odora*) is named for both its powerful fragrance and its rosy purple flowers that appear in late winter and very early spring. The cultivar **'Alba'** has off-white flowers; **'Aureo-marginata'** and **'Variegata'** both have yellow-bordered leaves. All three grow in zones 7-9 and will tolerate a bit of shade.

Rose daphne (*D. cneorum*) is a dainty low-growing shrub (about a foot high) that produces rose-pink flowers in mid-spring. The cultivar **'Eximea'** has somewhat larger, deep-pink flowers; **'Alba'** has white flowers; and **'Variegata'** has cream-edged leaves and rose-pink flowers. Rose daphne will also tolerate some shade, and it's hardy in zones 4-7—but it will usually lose at least some foliage in subzero weather.

Viburnums (*Viburnum* spp.) are medium-to-large shrubs with handsome dark green leaves, showy displays of white spring flowers, and red, blue, or black berries in summer, fall, and winter. **Leatherleaf viburnum** (*V. rhytidophyllum*) has lustrous, deeply wrinkled leaves, clusters of yellowish white flowers that are as much as eight inches across, and red berries that turn black and remain on the bush until early winter (if not eaten by birds). Leatherleaf viburnum will grow as high as fifteen feet. Its range is zones 5-7, but it'll lose its foliage at minus ten degrees Fahrenheit, so it's reliably evergreen only in zones 7-9. The compact **David viburnum** (*V. davidii*) grows to just three to five feet tall and has deeply veined leaves, two- to-three-inch wide clusters of white flowers, and showy blue berries. Its range is zones 8-9. **Laurustinus** (*V. tinus*) has lustrous, almost black-green leaves, fragrant white flowers in early spring, and metallic blue-black berries. It's hardy in zones 8-10 and grows eight to ten feet high. **'Eve Price'** and **'Spring Bouquet'** are compact varieties with smaller leaves and pinkish-white flowers.

Hardy in zones 7-10, **Japanese aucuba** (*Aucuba japonica*) is valued not for its inconspicuous flowers but for its large, showy scarlet berries, which appear in the fall and remain on the plant through the winter, and especially for the beautiful variegated leaves of many of its cultivars, which provide year-round color. **'Crotonifolia,'** for example, has white flecks on green leaves; **'Picturata'** has a large splotch of yellow in the middle of its spotted green leaves; **'Sulphur'** sports leaves with wide golden-yellow edges and dark-green centers; and **'Variegata,'** known as **gold dust plant,** has lovely gold-flecked green leaves. A large but slow-growing shrub, aucuba will prosper even in deep shade. To have berries, however, you need more light, as well as a female plant to produce the berries and a male plant to fertilize them.

The greatest strength of **thorny eleagnus,** or **silverberry** (*Eleagnus pungens*), isn't its tiny whitish autumn flowers or its red spring berries but the lovely foliage of its variegated cultivars. The leaves of **'Variegata'** have elegant white or yellow margins; **'Aurea'** has gold-edged foliage; and the large leaves of **'Maculata,'** perhaps the most beautiful cultivar of all, have golden yellow blotches in their centers. Hardy in zones 7-10, thorny eleagnus tolerates shade and grows quickly to as high as fifteen feet.

Like thorny eleagnus, **Japanese euonymus** (*Euonymus japonica*) is renowned not for its nearly inconspicuous flowers or even its red autumn berries but for the large colorful leaves of its many variegated cultivars. The foliage of **'Silver Knight,'** for example, has creamy white borders; the leaves of **'Matanzaki'** are edged in golden yellow. Japanese euonymus grows relatively fast to as high as fifteen feet, it's shade tolerant, and it grows in zones 7-9.

Another shade-tolerant shrub is **Japanese aralia,** or **Japanese fatsia** (*Fatsia japonica*, also known as *Aralia japonica* or *Aralia sieboldiana*). This impressive shrub produces small black berries in the fall and large, showy clusters of tiny milky-white flowers in fall and winter, when practically nothing else is in bloom. It also has impressive tropical-looking foliage—glossy dark-green, deeply loped leaves as much as sixteen inches wide. The leaves of **'Variegata'** and **'Aurea'** are especially valuable because they have golden or cream-colored variegation. Japanese aralia can quickly grow as high as ten feet. It's hardy in zones 7-10, but may flower only in zones 8-10.

Fatshedera (*Fatsia japonica* x *Fatshedera lizei*) is a cross between Japanese aralia and English ivy. It has the flower clusters of the shrub and the large pointed-lobed leaves and vinelike climbing habit of the ivy. It's also shade loving, fast growing to six feet high, and suitable for zones 7-10. At least two cultivars have variegated white or yellow foliage.

Like most hollies, **Silver Edge English holly** (*Ilex aquifolium* 'Silver Edge') produces only inconspicuous flowers. Unlike most other hollies, however, it can create color not only with its red berries but also with its pretty white-edged leaves. It grows slowly to between twenty and thirty feet tall, and its range is zones 7-9. Unfortunately, it does well only in cool, moist climates like the Pacific Northwest.

Nandina, or **heavenly bamboo** (*Nandina domestica*), which isn't a bamboo at all, is treasured for its long clusters of small, creamy-white spring flowers, its equally large clusters of big bright-red berries, its purplish-red or coppery new foliage, and its striking bronze or purplish fall and winter foliage. The cultivar **'Alba'** has white berries; the dwarf **'Atropurpurea Nana'** has rich red winter foliage. Heavenly bamboo is hardy in zones 6-9, but it will stay evergreen only in Zones 7-9. It grows slowly to six or eight feet tall and it will tolerate some shade—though its foliage won't be as colorful as it is in full sun.

Hardy in zones 7-9, **Japanese ternstroemia** (*Ternstroemia gymnanthera*) has lustrous leaves that are deep green in the shade (which the plant tolerates nicely) and almost purple in full sun. It also produces tiny creamy flowers in the summer, followed by red and yellow berries.

Also hardy in zones 7-9, **Chinese fringe flower** (*Loropetalum chinense*) is a large, irregular shrub with showy masses of white witch hazel-like flowers in spring.

Leatherleaf mahonia (*Mahonia bealei*) has the prickly ivylike leaves, yellow flowers, and blue-black berries of its cousin, Oregon grape (see page 48), but it grows much taller—up to twelve feet. Its range, however, is only zones 7-9.

Photinia is known for its clusters of small white spring flowers, its red berries, and especially its shiny foliage, which is red when new. **Chinese photinia** (*P. serrulata*) grows to between ten and thirty feet high, **Japanese photinia** (*P. glabra*) reaches twelve feet high, and **Fraser photinia** (*P. x fraseri*), a hybrid of the two that's also known as **redtop** (after its new foliage), grows to fifteen feet. Japanese and Fraser photinia have the reddest new leaves, and their range is zones 7-9. Chinese photinia grows in zones 6-9.

If you live in or south of Zone 8 (most of which is in the Deep South or on the West Coast), your evergreen palette is even larger.

It includes **camellias,** a genus of tall shrubs that produces dense glossy foliage and large white, pink, or red flowers from fall to spring; the delicate blossoms provide rare and welcome color during the coolest months of the year (photograph, page 58). **Common camellias,** or **Japanese camellias** (*Camellia japonica*), can reach twenty feet and bloom from late fall through early spring. **Sasanqua camellias** (*C. Sasanqua*) grow six to ten feet tall and bloom from early fall to early winter. Although camellias are hardy in zones 7-9, they do best in regions without heavy frosts, which can damage their flowers. They also prefer light shade.

Gardenias (*Gardenia jasminoides*) are grown for their shiny dark-green leaves and elegant, highly fragrant, pure-white two- to four-inch-wide flowers that bloom from spring to summer. The cultivars **'August Beauty'** and **'Veitchii'** bloom from spring to fall. All three shrubs grow to between four and six feet tall. Other cultivars, such as **'Radicans'** and **'Prostrata,'** are much smaller. Although gardenias grow in zones 8-10, long periods of frost (likely in zones 8-9) will damage their foliage.

Hardy in zones 8-11, **oleander** (*Nerium oleander*) produces masses of inch-wide flowers—white, red, rose, or pink, depending on the variety—all summer long and well into the fall. It's also a tough (and poisonous) shrub that will tolerate less-than-ideal growing conditions and will quickly grow as tall as twenty feet.

The handsome and graceful **Tobira,** or **Japanese pittosporum** (*Pittosporum tobira*), has creamy-yellow spring flowers that smell like orange blossoms and leathery lemon-scented, dark-green paddle-shaped leaves that make it look like pachysandra (see page 68) growing upright. One of several variegated cultivars, **'Variegatum'** has cream-edged gray-green leaves that resemble variegated pachysandra. Both shrubs grow as high as fifteen feet and are hardy in zones 8-10. In contrast, the dense **'Wheeler's Dwarf'** grows to only three feet and is hardy in zones 9-10.

Reaching as high as twelve feet, **San Diego ceanothus** (*Ceanothus cyaneus* 'Sierra Blue') is often called "wild lilac" because its large showy cone-shaped clusters of lavender-blue spring flowers bear a striking resemblance to lilac blossoms (*Syringa* spp.). The related **Carmel creeper** (*C. griseus horizontalis*) is a much smaller shrub with smaller, rounded flower clusters. Both plants grow in zones 8-10.

Hardy in zones 8-10, **Raphiolepis** is a genus of medium-size shrubs with leathery leaves and showy clusters of pink or white spring flowers. The species **Indian Hawthorn** (*R. indica*) has pinkish white flowers. **Yeddo raphiolepis** (*R. umbellata*) has very thick leaves, fragrant white flowers, and black berries; the cultivar **'Springtime'** is especially valuable because it produces pink flowers from January to April.

Three more colorful evergreen shrubs are also hardy in zones 8-10: **Mexican orange** (*Choiya ternata*), which has smooth shiny leaves and small, fragrant white spring flowers; **Easter broom** (*Cytisus racemosus*), which has long clusters of yellow spring flowers; and **common flannel bush** (*Fremontodendron californicum*), also known as **leatherwood, mountain leatherwood,** and **slippery elm**, which produces an abundance of large (one-and-one-half-inch-wide) showy, cup-shaped flowers in spring.

If you live in zones 9-10 (most of which is in California, Florida, and along the Gulf Coast) you can grow two more fine-looking evergreens.

The most beautiful is **Brazil raintree** (*Brunfelsia pauciflora*), a low-spreading shrub with large, delicate-looking lavender flowers from spring to summer. Its cultivar **Yesterday, Today, and Tomorrow** (*B. pauciflora* 'Floribunda') is a much taller bush with an unusual trait: Over a three-day period, its flowers change color from purple to lavender and white, thereby creating an unusually pleasing combination of three different-colored blossoms at the same time. Both shrubs will take partial shade.

Sweet-pea shrub (*Polygala* x *dalmaisiana*), which grows to between three and six feet tall, produces striking bright red-pink flowers for several weeks in the spring.

If you live in Zone 10, which is mainly South Florida and the California coast, you can grow **Natal plum**, or **Amatungula** (*Carissa grandiflora*), which has fragrant five-petaled white flowers year round and large (one- to two-inch-wide) egg-shaped red fruits.

Deciduous shrubs

Deciduous shrubs have many limitations. Unlike evergreens, they can't provide year round color; on the contrary, in cold-winter climates they're bare much of the year, so they're not good for privacy screens. Unlike deciduous trees, their branches are usually much too small to create an imposing winter silhouette. Moreover, their foliage is rarely as attractive as that of evergreen shrubs, and it's seldom variegated. Many deciduous shrubs, however, *can* perform a valuable function that many plants cannot: Their flowers and fruits can provide bursts of color in summer, fall, and winter, after most plants have already bloomed.

Several deciduous **azaleas** (*Rhododendron* spp.), for example, flower in late June or July. **'Golden Showers'** has peachy-yellow flowers, and its glossy green leaves turn bronze in the fall. **'Innocence'** produces fragrant masses of small white blossoms, and its slightly bronzy foliage turns burgundy red in the autumn. The pale yellow flowers of **'Lemon Drop'** have a slight lemon scent, and its blue-green foliage turns red in the fall. The flowers of **'Lollipop'** are pink at first, then silver-pink. **'Parade'** has dark pink flowers with an orange eye, and **'Pink 'n Sweet'** has pink blossoms with a lighter pink-and-yellow center. All are hardy in zones 4-9.

Among the most colorful deciduous shrubs in cold-winter climates are **hydrangeas** (*Hydrangea* spp.)—vigorous plants with large, coarse dark-green leaves and unusually large white, pink, or blue flower clusters that bloom for weeks in July, August, and even September, when most other shrubs have shed their blossoms. **Bigleaf hydrangeas** (*H. macrophylla*), with large, six- to ten-inch flower clusters, are among the showiest. The cultivar **'Nikko Blue'** has big, globe-shaped clusters of blue flowers in July and August. (Flowers will be pink in less-acid soil; you can add aluminum sulphate to make it more acidic.) **Pink Beauty** (*H. macrophylla* 'Pink') has pink flowers and dark-red new stems. **Red Flower** (*H. macrophylla* 'Alpenguhlen') has reddish-purple blossoms. All grow to four or five feet. **Blue Lacecap** (*H. macrophylla* 'Coerulea'), which grows three to six feet tall, has deep-blue flower clusters that resemble a lacy pinwheel. The unusual **Variegated Lacecap Hydrangea** (*H. macrophylla* 'Variegata'), which grows as high as three feet, has blue to pink flowers (depending on soil pH) and creamy-white margins on its leaves. All bigleaf hydrangeas grow in zones 6-9.

Panicle hydrangeas (*H. paniculata*) are even taller than the bigleaf types—ten to fifteen feet; they have even larger flower clusters—sometimes a foot long or longer; they bloom even later—well into September—and they're the hardiest hydrangeas of all, growing in zones 3-8. They're not, how-ever, as colorful as the bigleafs. The fast-growing **P. G. Hydrangea** (*H. paniculata* 'Grandiflora') blossoms in August and September; its flowers are cream-colored, then bronzy-pink, then brown. As its name suggests, the **P. G. Hydrangea Tree** (*H. paniculata* 'Grandiflora' tree form) can be shaped into a small tree, with a crown.

Oakleaf hydrangea (*H. quercifolia*) has white flowers that later turn purplish pink, then brown; and—unusual for hydrangeas—it produces orange-brown, red, and purple fall foliage. It grows four to six feet tall and is hardy in zones 5-9.

All hydrangeas can tolerate some shade (albeit with fewer flowers), but **smooth hydrangea** (*H. arborescens*), which has large white or creamy-white flowers, can tolerate it best of all. It's range is zones 4-9.

Rose-of-Sharon (*Hibiscus syriacus*) is a large, five- to twelve-foot-high shrub that produces masses of three- to four-inch-wide saucer-shaped flowers from July until frost. Its many varieties sport single and double red, white, blue, pink, rose, and lavender blossoms. It's hardy in zones 5-8 and will tolerate some shade (but with fewer flowers).

The tough, fast-growing **rugosa,** or **beach rose** (*Rosa rugosa*), produces fragrant two- to three-inch-wide pink or deep-red flowers in early summer and more sporadic blossoms all summer long. The flowers are followed by deep-red fruits known as rose hips and by yellow or orange foliage in the fall. The cultivar **'Alba'** has white flowers. Rugosas can grow about six feet high and more than twice as wide. They also have a wide range—zones 2-7.

Potentilla, or **bush cinquefoil** (*Potentilla fruticosa*), puts out lots of showy flowers in spring and somewhat fewer blossoms throughout the summer. Most of its cultivars sport yellow flowers that resemble buttercups. **'Princess,'** however, has pink flowers, **'Red Ace'** has red-orange blossoms, and **'Abbotswood'** has white flowers. All potentillas are undemanding shrubs that grow slowly to two to four feet tall, and they're hardy throughout zones 2-6.

Glossy abelia (*Abelia* x *grandiflora*) produces small but showy soft-pink trumpet-shaped flowers from June through fall; it also has lustrous dark-green leaves that become a striking bronze-red or bronze-purple in the fall. **Edward Goucher glossy abelia** (*A.* 'Edward Goucher') has rosy lavender flowers. Both shrubs reach three to five feet, and they can tolerate light shade. They're hardy in zones 6-9 and evergreen in zones 8-9.

The well-named **summersweet** (*Clethra alnifolia*), also known as **sweet pepperbush** or **spiked alder,** has creased deep green leaves, extremely fragrant clusters, or "spikes," of tiny white flowers in July and August, and pale-yellow to rich golden-brown (and sometimes orange) foliage in the fall. The species grows four to eight feet tall. Two cultivars, 'Hummingbird' and **Compact** (*C. alnifolia* 'Compacta'), however, grow only three or four feet high; 'Hummingbird' has lustrous black-green leaves and more prolific flowers. **Pink summersweet** (*C. alnifolia* 'Rosea') has pale pink blossoms that gradually turn white. Hardy in zones 4-9, summersweet does well in moist soils and tolerates some shade.

Virginia sweetspire (*Itea virginica*) produces striking narrow, six-inch-long clusters of fragrant white flowers in the summer and red leaves in the fall. It grows three to five feet tall and thrives in zones 5-9.

Bottlebrush buckeye (*Aesculus parviflora*) is named for the pointed, eight- to twelve-inch-long clusters of tiny white flowers appearing on the bush in July that resemble bottlebrushes. Hardy in zones 4-8, the shrub also has pretty yellow foliage in the fall. It grows eight to twelve feet high and tolerates partial shade.

From July to September, **orange-eye butterfly bush** (*Buddleia davidii*) has five- to ten-inch-long clusters of tiny fragrant flowers that attract butterflies. Hardy in zones 5-9, the well-named shrub grows quickly to between ten and fifteen feet tall. Its many cultivars offer a rainbow of flower colors. 'White Profusion,' for example, sports bright white blossoms, 'Sun Gold' has golden yellow flowers, 'Royal Red' has rich purple-red blooms, and the blossoms of 'Black Knight' are vivid dark purple. 'Pink Delight' has clusters of deep-pink flowers that grow as long as fifteen inches, and 'Nanho Purple' is a spreading dwarf with magenta-purple flowers.

The long, arching branches of **alternate-leaf butterfly bush,** or **fountain buddleia** (*B. alternifolia*), are covered with clusters of lilac-purple flowers in the summer. The cultivar 'Argentea' has silky-haired leaves with a silvery sheen. Both shrubs are large—ten to twenty feet tall—and their range is zones 5-7.

Buttonbush (*Cephalanthus occidentalis*) is named for the small round buttonlike clusters of fragrant creamy-white flowers that appear on the shrub in June, July, and August. This moisture-loving shrub has lustrous bright-green creased foliage that turns a peachy orange-yellow in autumn. Hardy over a wide range—zones 5-11—buttonbush grows three to six feet tall.

Other deciduous shrubs that are hardy in cold climates are valued not only for their flowers but for their colorful, long-lasting foliage or berries.

Some **spireas**, for example, have summer flowers, others have summer-long yellow foliage, and still others have both. **Japanese white spirea** (*Spirea albiflora*) is a low-spreading, one- to two-foot-high shrub with large clusters of white flowers in June and July. **Anthony Waterer Spirea** (*S.* x *bumalda* 'Anthony Waterer') is a three- to four-foot-high bush with four- to six-inch-wide clusters of carmine-pink flowers from June to August. Its new foliage is reddish purple with pink highlights; then it turns deep green and in the fall becomes reddish purple again. Another cultivar, **dwarf red flowering spirea** (*S.* x *bumalda* 'Coccinea'), produces deep bluish-green foliage and crimson flowers in June and July. 'Goldflame' has pink flowers, variegated red, copper, and orange foliage in the spring and fall, and greenish-yellow leaves in the summer. One of the most colorful cultivars is 'Goldmound,' which bears fine yellow leaves from spring to fall and pink flowers in July and August. All these shrubs grow in zones 3-8.

Hardy in zones 4-8, the dainty, wide-spreading **Daphne spirea** (*S. japonica* 'Alpina'—so named because it resembles an alpine flower) grows just one foot high. It has fine-textured blue-green foliage and three-inch-wide clusters of light pink flowers in June and July. 'Little Princess' is a two- to three-foot-high cultivar with rose-pink flowers from midsummer to fall and deep-red autumn leaves.

Blue Mist Spirea, also known as **Bluebeard,** is not really a spirea, but *Caryopteris* x *clandonensis*. It produces erect clusters of powder-blue flowers from August until the first frost. **Dark Knight Blue Mist Spirea** (*C.* x *clandonensis* 'Dark Knight') has blue-purple flowers. Hardy in zones 6-9, both plants have gray-green foliage and grow two to three feet high.

All **weigelas** (*Weigela florida*) have showy trumpet-shaped late-spring flowers, but several of its many cultivars also have colorful summer foliage. The three- to five-foot-tall '**Java Red,**' for instance, has both deep pink blossoms and dark purple leaves. '**Minuet,**' which grows two to three feet tall, has variegated yellow, lilac, and ruby-red flowers and green leaves tinged with purple. **Variegated weigela** (*W. florida* 'Variegata') grows five to seven feet tall and has rose-pink flowers and green leaves edged with yellow or creamy white. '**Red Prince**' produces red flowers in the spring and sometimes a second bloom in late summer. All these cultivars grow in zones 5-8, except for 'Red Prince,' whose range is zones 5-6.

American elder, or **American elderberry** (*Sambucus canadensis*), has six- to ten-inch-wide clusters of tiny white flowers in June, followed by purple-black berries that can be used to make jelly or wine. Several cultivars have gold leaves, including '**Aurea,**' which also produces cherry-red berries and grows six to twelve feet high. American elder has a wide range: zones 4-9.

Golden Vicary Privet (*Ligustrum* x *vicaryi*) has clusters of white flowers in the spring and, more important, dense bright-yellow foliage as long as the shrub is in full sun. Like all privets, this one is tough, fast growing, and tolerant of both pollution and drought. Hardy in zones 5-8, it grows ten to twelve feet high.

Purple-leaf sand cherry (*Prunus* x *cistena*) is covered with small, fragrant pinkish flowers in late spring and early summer. What makes this shrub especially valuable, however, is its rich deep-purple foliage (photograph, page 49). It's also one of the hardiest purple-leaf plants—its range is zones 3-7—and it grows eight to ten feet tall.

The **purple giant filbert** (*Corylus maxima*) is treasured not for its inconspicuous flowers but for its striking creased dark-purple leaves (which unfortunately slowly fade to dark-green in the summer). This sometimes treelike shrub grows ten to twenty feet tall and it's hardy in zones 4-7. The cooler the climate, the longer the leaves stay purple.

Similarly, **Japanese barberries** are valued not for their tiny flowers but for the red or gold foliage of certain cultivars and the masses of bright-red berries that last all winter. **Red-leaved Japanese barberry** (*Berberis thunbergii atropurpurea*), which grows three to six feet tall (photograph, page 49), and the cultivar '**Crimson Pygmy,**' which grows less than two feet, both have deep-red or purple leaves. The foliage of '**Rosy Glow,**' which grows five to six feet high, is rose-pink mottled with maroon when it's new and maroon-red when it's older. The dense, slow-growing **golden barberry** (*B. thunbergii* 'Aurea'), which has vivid yellow leaves, eventually reaches three or four feet high. '**Gold Ring,**' which grows to five or six feet, has deep-red or purple leaves like red-leaved barberry, but with a distinct gold border. All five shrubs are hardy in zones 4-8.

The popular **burning bush** (*Euonymus alatus*) is prized not for its unremarkable flowers or even its tiny berries but for its uncommonly brilliant red fall foliage. The species is big—it can eventually reach fifteen to twenty feet in both height and width. **Dwarf burning bush** (*E. alatus* 'Compactus') is a relatively low eight to ten feet and '**Angelica**' only six feet. All three shrubs grow in zones 4-8.

Common winterberry (*Ilex verticillata*) is most valuable for its masses of red berries. They're more profuse than on any other holly, and they can actually make the plant look red in the winter. The species has deep-green leaves and is hardy in zones 3-9. The cultivar '**Afterglow**' has orange or orange-red berries and grows in zones 4-9. Both shrubs reach six to ten feet high. '**Harvest Red**' has deep-red berries and lustrous dark-green leaves that turn deep reddish purple in the fall. It's hardy in zones 3-9 and grows ten to twelve feet high. The dense, compact '**Red Sprite,**' which grows only two or three feet tall, produces tiny white flowers and large, half-inch-wide red berries. The shade-tolerant '**Winter Red**' grows six to nine feet high and has lustrous dark-green leaves and bright-red berries. Both 'Red Sprite' and 'Winter Red' are hardy in zones 4-9.

Red chokeberry (*Aronia arbutifolia* 'Brilliantissima') produces masses of white flower clusters in the spring and glossy dark-green leaves. It's named, however, for its brilliant scarlet fall foliage and even more brilliant glossy red berries that last into the winter. The cultivar grows as high as ten feet, and its range is zones 4-9.

How to Create Privacy, Color, and Interest . . .

If you live in or south of Zone 6, you can grow **winter jasmine** (*Jasminum nudiflorum*), which is named for the fact that its thin, arching branches are covered with small yellow flowers in late winter or very early spring. The species has lustrous deep-green leaves, grows four or five feet tall, and is hardy in zones 6-10. The leaves of the cultivar '**Aureum**' have yellow blotches; the leaves of '**Variegatum**' have white margins.

Hardy in zones 6-11, **swamp cyrilla,** or **leatherwood** (*Cyrilla racemiflora*), is known for its six-inch-long twiglike clusters of showy yellow flowers in the summer and shiny, pointed dark-green leaves that turn orange or red in the fall.

If you live in zones 7-10, you can grow an even larger variety of attractive summer-flowering shrubs.

Lilac chastetree (*Vitex agnus-castus*) is named for its footlong, roughly lilaclike pointed clusters of tiny fragrant lilacblue flowers. There are also white- and pink-flowered cultivars, most of which, like the species, are hardy in zones 6-8 and grow between seven and twenty feet tall. The related **chastetree** (*V. negundo*) has shorter clusters of pinkish flowers, usually grows ten to fifteen feet tall, and is hardy in zones 6-8.

California tree poppy, or matilija poppy (*Romneya coulteri*), which grows to eight feet high, is celebrated for its showy flowers: elegant white blossoms with yellow centers that are as much as six inches across.

Crimson-spot rockrose (*Cistus landaniferus*) reaches about four feet tall and produces showy white three- to four-inch-wide flowers, each with a distinctive pattern of five purplish blotches arranged in a pentagon shape around a yellow center, or eye.

If you live in zones 8-10, you can also grow two other rockroses—so called because they're often planted in rock gardens. **Orchid rockrose** (*C. x purpureus*), which grows three to four feet high, has the same purple blotches and yellow centers as crimson-spot rockrose but produces two- to three-inch-wide pinkish red flowers instead of white ones. *C. x pulverulentus* grows only two feet tall and produces inch-wide purple flowers with dull orange-yellow eyes, but no blotches.

Also hardy in zones 8-10 is **Spanish broom** (*Spartium junceum*), a six- to eight-foot-tall shrub whose long, thin stalks are decorated, and often covered, with small bright-yellow flowers from summer to fall.

If you live in zones 9-10, you can grow **princess flower** (*Tibouchina urvilleana*), which produces pretty velvety green leaves and showy, vivid-purple three- to four-inch-wide flowers year round.

Evergreen Ground Covers

Evergreen ground covers are low, spreading plants that provide year-round interest. While shrubs and trees are the walls and ceilings of the outdoor room, ground covers are the carpet. Plant them between and in front of trees and shrubs, where they'll be easily seen. Also use them in narrow places where larger plants can't fit. To bring as much color as possible into your yard, choose ground covers with not just one colorful feature—flowers, berries, or foliage—but several. The traditional ground cover is a lawn. These ground covers are much more interesting, and, unlike grass, they require almost no care.

Many colorful ground covers are hardy in cold-winter climates. Among the prettiest is **vinca** (*Vinca minor*), also known as **periwinkle, myrtle,** or **creeping myrtle.** (photographs, pages 50 and 53-54) Hardy in zones 4-8, this fast-growing spreader makes a thick carpet, rarely more than six inches high, of small glossy dark-green or variegated leaves, and produces a large bouquet of bright five-petaled flowers in April and May. The species, known simply as **vinca** or **blue myrtle,** has bluish-lavender blossoms; '**Bowles Variety**' has larger, deeper blue flowers; '**Burgundy**' has deep-red flowers; **white myrtle** (*V. minor* 'Alba,') produces bright-white flowers; and **purple myrtle** (*V. minor* 'Atropurpurea,') has reddish-purple blossoms. Among the variegated varieties, '**Argenteovariegata**' has blue flowers and green-and-white foliage; '**Sterling Silver**' has lavender-blue flowers and green-and-white leaves. Vinca does best in light shade but will tolerate both sunlight and full shade.

As its name suggests, **big periwinkle** (*Vinca major*) is larger than vinca minor. It grows between one and two feet high, its leaves can reach two or three inches long, and its blue flowers are one to two inches wide. The leaves of the justly popular cultivar **'Variegata'** have creamy white margins. Unfortunately, big periwinkle is hardy only in zones 6-9.

Bearberry, or **kinnikinick** (*Arctostaphylos uva-ursi*) resembles a very low cotoneaster. Small, leathery, glossy green leaves cover long, thin branches that may eventually spread fifteen feet or more but rarely grow more than a foot high. Clusters of tiny bell-shaped flowers—waxy white blossoms with a touch of pink that resemble lily-of-the-valley—appear in April or May, and lustrous red berries emerge in late summer. In the fall its leaves turn reddish or bronzy. Bearberry is very hardy (zones 2-6) and it can tolerate some shade.

Mountain cranberry (*Vaccinium vitis-idaea minus*) is not a cranberry but a relative of the blueberry. It produces clusters of tiny, pinkish-white flowers similar to bearberry's in May and June and dark-red berries in August; in the winter its tiny, lustrous dark-green leaves turn a rich mahogany. Mountain cranberry is a very low shrub, barely four inches high, and it spreads slowly by underground runners. Hardy in zones 3-5, it grows best in full sun.

Wintergreen (*Gaultheria procumbens*), also called **checkerberry** or **teaberry,** produces modest white or pinkish flowers from spring to fall, glossy green foliage that turns a beautiful reddish purple in the winter, and edible bright scarlet berries that stay on the plant from midsummer until the following spring. Rarely more than six inches tall, wintergreen prefers light shade and grows in zones 3-5.

Like other ivies (photographs, pages 57-58), **English ivy** (*Hedera helix*) has shiny lobed leaves two to four inches long. Like many ivies, it can be very slow starting, especially in shade; but after it's established it grows swiftly and aggressively. It also tolerates heavy shade, and it's hardy in zones 4-9. English ivy doesn't bear colorful fruits or flowers, but several cultivars have lovely variegated foliage. Among the most beautiful is **'Gold Heart,'** whose dark-green leaves have a large warm splotch of creamy white in the center. **'Buttercup'** and **'Sulphurea'** have green-and-gold leaves, and **'Glacier'** has green leaves with thin white margins.

Like English ivy, **wintercreeper** (*Euonymus fortunei*) toler-

ates shade, and it provides color not with its inconspicuous flowers or fruits but with its very small oval leaves that turn red in winter. Its variegated cultivars include **'Harlequin'** and **'Silver Queen,'** which have creamy-white-and-green leaves; **'Variegatus'** and **'Sunspot,'** whose foliage is yellow and green; and **'Gracilis,'** whose green-and-white leaves have a pink tinge in winter. Wintercreeper grows slowly but steadily and, like ivy, is hardy in zones 5-8.

Both English ivy and wintercreeper are vines (see below). Unless you're prepared to cut them back periodically, don't plant them near things you don't want them to climb.

Like English ivy and wintercreeper, **pachysandra** (*Pachysandra terminalis*) lacks showy flowers or foliage. It is, however, a tough, reliable plant that grows in zones 4-8 and creates a smooth, solid carpet of shiny, dark-green foliage even in deep shade. Its variegated cultivar **'Silver Edge'** has narrow white leaf margins that can bring a bit of color into the darkest parts of the garden.

Many evergreen ground covers are sun-loving herbs or herblike plants with very small, often very narrow leaves that form thick, sometimes grasslike mats of foliage year round.

One of the most popular—and justifiably so—is **ground phlox** (*Phlox subulata*), also known as **ground pink, moss pink,** or **moss phlox.** For nearly a month in late spring or early summer the entire plant is a sheet of bright color (photograph, page 54). The wider the plant spreads, the wider the sweep of color. The cultivar **'White Delight'** has white flowers, **'Red Wings'** has red blossoms, **'Emerald Blue'** and **'Millstream Jupiter'** have blue flowers, **'Millstream Laura'** has pale pink blossoms, and **'Millstream Daphne'** has rosy-pink flowers. Hardy in zones 3-9, ground phlox is tough and fast growing.

Like ground phlox, **Snow-in-summer** (*Cerastium tomentosum*) is vigorous, fast growing, and hardy in zones 3-9. It's covered with small white flowers from late spring to summer and has striking light-gray woolly foliage.

Evergreen candytuft (*Iberis sempervirens*) produces dense mats of dark-green foliage and showy one- to two-inch-wide clusters of tiny white flowers in the spring. It grows as high as a foot and is hardy in zones 4-8.

How to Create Privacy, Color, and Interest . . .

Spring cinquefoil (*Potentilla verna*, also known as *P. tabernaemontani*) has bright-yellow spring flowers and dark-green strawberrylike toothed leaves that form a mat three to six inches high. **Alpine cinquefoil** (*P. cinerea*) has pale pink flowers and four-inch-high foliage. *P. nepalensis* 'Willmottiae' has striking deep red flowers and grows up to ten inches high. **Three-toothed cinquefoil** (*P. tridentata*) grows up to nine inches and produces small white flowers and shiny dark-green leaves that turn maroon in the fall. All cinquefoils grow quickly, and their range is zones 3-9—except for spring cinquefoil, which grows in zones 4-9.

Barren strawberry (*Waldsteinia* spp.) also has strawberrylike foliage and showy bright-yellow spring flowers. Hardy in zones 4-9, *W. ternata* grows up to four inches high. *W. fragarioides* reaches four to ten inches and grows in zones 5-9.

Sun rose (*Helianthemum nummularium*), also known as **rock rose** or **frost weed,** produces showy single or double flowers one to two inches across for a long period in spring or early summer. Among its many cultivars are **'Firedragon,'** which has red-orange flowers; **'Wisley Pink,'** with pale pink blossoms; and **'Raspberry Ripple,'** which has pink-and-white flowers. If the flowers are cut back, the plant may bloom again in the fall. Rockroses grow six to eight inches high; their range is Zones 5-8.

Moss sandwort (*Arenaria verna*) is a slow-growing, widespreading, moisture-loving herb with clusters of tiny white flowers in the spring and fine, grasslike foliage that rarely grows more than three inches high. It's also extremely hardy, thriving in zones 2-10. Its cultivar **'Aurea'** offers a bonus: yellow-green foliage.

Irish moss, or **Pearlwort** (*Sagina subulata*), is a mosslike creeper, seldom more than four inches tall, dotted with tiny white flowers in the spring. **Scotch moss** (*S. subulata* 'Aurea') has golden-green foliage. Both plants grow in zones 5-8 and, unlike other plants in this group, can thrive in shade.

Thift, or **sea pink** (*Armeria maritima*), produces clumps of dark-green needlelike foliage that resembles chives, as well as small white or rose-pink flowers in spring and early summer. The cultivar **'Californica'** has larger flowers, **'Alba'** has white flowers, and **'Purpurea'** produces purple blossoms. All are low, slow growing, and very hardy—zones 2-10.

Mossy or **gold-moss stonecrop** (*Sedum acre*), which grows in zones 4-10, produces a two- to five-inch-high mat of light-green foliage, as well as yellow flowers in mid- to late spring. The fast-growing *S. sarmentosum* (zones 3-10) produces a six-inch-high mat of yellow-green foliage and masses of bright-yellow flowers.

Several herb or herblike evergreen ground covers are especially useful because they bloom in summer, when few plants of any kind are blooming.

Hardy in zones 5-8, **germander** (*Teucrium chamaedys*) has small rose or lavender flowers and dark-green foliage as much as a foot high.

Mother-of-thyme, or **creeping thyme** (*Thymus serphyllum*), has tiny rounded dark-green foliage that grows to six inches and clusters of minute dark-pink flowers. **White creeping thyme** (*T. serphyllym* 'Albus') has white flowers and shorter foliage. **Pink creeping thyme** (*T. serphyllum* 'Roseus') has pink blossoms. Hardy in zones 4-8, all these plants are vigorous and aromatic, especially when touched. They're also spices.

Some forms of the tough, fast-spreading **stonecrop** bloom in the summer. **Shortleaf stonecrop** (*Sedum album,* sometimes called *S. brevifolium*) has white flowers and grayish foliage with a red blush. It grows three to six inches high, and its range is zones 4-10. **English stonecrop** (*S. anglicum*) also has white flowers and grows in zones 4-10, but it's seldom taller than three inches. **Yellow stonecrop** (*S. reflexum*), hardy in zones 5-8, produces three-inch-high gray-green foliage and golden-yellow flowers on foot-high stems. *S. dasyphyllum* has very low (one- to two-inch-high) bluish-green foliage and white flowers in summer and fall. Its range is zones 7-10.

The vigorous **two-row stonecrop** (*S. spurium,* also called *S. stoloniferum*) has pink flowers in July and August and three- to six-inch-high foliage that turns red in winter. The variety **'Dragon's Blood'** has deep-rose-red flowers, and the margins of its mature foliage are tinged bronzy purple. **'Tricolor'** has striking green-and-white foliage with splashes of red. **'Splendens'** has deep carmine flowers. Two-row stonecrop grows in zones 3-10, but in colder climates it's only semievergreen.

Other evergreen sedums are hardy only in the mild-winter climates of zones 8-10. Among the most colorful is **pork and beans,** or **whiskey nose** (*S.* x *rubrotinctum*), named for its beanlike green leaves that become bright-bronzy-red in full sun. Whiskey nose grows three to six inches high and has yellow spring flowers. *S. oaxacanum* also has yellow spring flowers, as well as six-inch-tall grayish-green foliage. *S. palmeri (compressum)* produces six- to eight-inch-high gray-green foliage and yellow flowers from April to June. The foot-high *S. confusum* has light-green leaves and yellow flowers in the summer.

Vines

On small lots, where privacy must be created by walls, fences, and overhead structures such as pergolas (see pages 27-28), *evergreen* vines are invaluable. They can climb up privacy barriers to hide, soften, and decorate them year round. They can also create additional year-round privacy by growing even taller than a fence or wall (with proper support) and by growing between the joists, and thereby filling in the spaces, on top of a pergola.

Deciduous vines are especially useful on pergolas and other overhead structures that are designed not for privacy but for shade. A deciduous vine will provide shade only when it's needed—in warm weather, when the vine has leafed out, not in the winter, when the vine is bare.

Unlike other deciduous plants, deciduous vines won't leave a big bare spot in the ground in the winter, for vines grow mostly above ground. Even the tallest ones take up only a little bit of space *on* the ground, and even that little can usually be hidden behind another plant.

Any vine can provide color—with flowers, berries, and/or foliage—in the upper levels of the garden, where the only other colorful plants are flowering trees.

Unfortunately, only three vines are evergreen in cold-winter climates: **English ivy, wintercreeper,** and **cross vine.** All three can climb even flat structures such as walls and board fences because they climb not by twisting around things, as some other vines do, but by clinging directly to them with tiny rootlets on their branches. The fast-growing English ivy can climb as high as forty feet; wintercreeper can reach twenty feet.

Unlike wintercreeper or ivy (described on page 68), **cross vine** (*Bignonia capreolata*) doesn't have variegated leaves, but it does have clusters of lovely trumpet-shaped spring flowers. These two-inch-wide blossoms are variegated brownish, yellow, and orange. Cross vine also has pointed leathery dark-green leaves that become purplish in cold weather. It grows as high as fifty feet; and, like ivy and wintercreeper, it doesn't mind shade, but it flowers best in full sun. Unfortunately, it grows only in zones 6-9. It's named, incidentally, for this characteristic: When you cut through its woody stems, the pulpy tissue in the center of the cut is cross-shaped.

Cold-hardy deciduous vines

Perhaps the most colorful and picturesque deciduous vine is **wisteria**, a twining plant known for its massive twisting woody trunks and stunning chains of fragrant spring flowers.

Growing in zones 5-9, **Japanese wisteria** (*Wisteria floribunda*) produces twelve- to eighteen-inch-long chains of violet or bluish-violet flowers. **Pink Japanese wisteria** (*W. floribunda* 'Rosea') has eighteen-inch-long clusters of pink flowers. **Blue Japanese wisteria** (*W. floribunda* 'Issai') has foot-long deep-blue flower clusters. **'Alba'** has equally long chains of white flowers. **Double-flowering wisteria** (*W. floribunda* 'Plena') is named for its foot-long sprays of double violet blossoms. **Longcluster wisteria** (*W. floribunda macrobotrys*) produces chains of reddish-violet flowers that are two to three feet long, sometimes more.

Hardy in zones 5-8, **Chinese wisteria** (*W. sinensis*) sports bluish-violet flowers in foot-long chains. **White Chinese wisteria** (*W. sinensis alba*) is named for its white flowers, and **Jako Chinese wisteria** (*W. sinensis* 'Jako') has especially fragrant white blossoms. **Pink Chinese wisteria** (*W. sinensis* 'Rosea') has pink flowers, and **purple Chinese wisteria** (*W. sinensis* 'Purpurea') has purple blossoms.

The large-flowered hybrids of the **clematis** (*Clematis* var.) are known for their usually big, showy blossoms (actually petal-like sepals) that bloom from as early as May to as late as October. The five- to eight-inch-wide flowers include many different shades of pink, red, white, blue, and purple, as well as striking multicolored sepals. Dozens of different cultivars will grow anywhere from four to twenty feet tall. Choose those that will grow tall enough to cover whatever structures you want to mask.

Unlike the large-flowered hybrids, small-flowered clematis vines have wonderful fragrances. One of the showiest is **big-petal clematis,** or **downy clematis** (*C. macropetala*), which bears three- or four-inch wide pink or lavender flowers in the summer and grows to ten feet. **Anemone clematis** (*C. montana*), which has white, one-and-one-half to three-and-one-half-inch-wide flowers in the spring, is a vigorous woody vine that grows as high as twenty-five feet.

Clematis have dual personalities: They like cool, moist, shaded soil around their roots but lots of sun on their crowns. They're twining vines, so they can't climb a flat surface; they need a trellis or other support that they can twist around. The large-flowered selections grow in zones 4-8, the small-flowered ones in zones 5-7.

Trumpet vine, or trumpet creeper (*Campsis radicans*), is named for its clusters of orange-red trumpet-shaped flowers that blossom from June to October and most prolifically in midsummer, when few other plants are in bloom. The cultivars **'Apricot,' 'Flava,'** and **'Judy'** have yellow flowers; **'Crimson Trumpet'** and **'Praecox'** have red blossoms. Trumpet vines are tough woody plants that grow in zones 4-9 and quickly climb to between thirty and forty feet. **Madame Galen Trumpet Creeper** (*C. tagliabuana* 'Madame Galen') is similar, except it has salmon-red flowers and grows in zones 6-9. All trumpet creepers cling by rootlets, so they can climb almost anything. Their three-inch-long flowers also attract hummingbirds.

Honeysuckles are vigorous, fast-growing (some say invasive) vines with small decorative berries and little colorful tubular flowers. **Hall's honeysuckle** (*Lonicera japonica* 'Halliana') produces black berries and fragrant white flowers that turn yellow after they're fertilized; the vine usually has both white and yellow flowers at the same time. Flowering is profuse in early summer, then intermittent until fall. A woody vine that can grow thirty feet in one season, Hall's honeysuckle is semievergreen in the warmer regions of its range, which is zones 4-9. Although it grows much lower than other honeysuckles, the variety **Gold-net** (*L. japonica* 'Aureoreticulata') is especially valuable because of its variegated green-and-yellow leaves. **Goldflame honeysuckle** (*L.* x *heckrottii*) is named for its carmine-and-gold flowers that

bloom from June until frost (the carmine fades to pink). Hardy in zones 4-9, it produces red berries and grows ten to twenty feet high. **Dropmore scarlet honeysuckle** (*L.* x *brownii* 'Dropmore Scarlet') has red berries and orange-red flowers that bloom from June to September. Like goldflame honeysuckle, it also grows ten to twenty feet high, but its range is wider—zones 3-9. **Trumpet honeysuckle,** or **coral honeysuckle** (*L. sempervirens*), is named for its long, thin trumpet-shaped blossoms, which are bright orange or red outside and yellow inside and bloom from spring through summer. The cultivar **'Sulphurea'** has clear yellow flowers. Trumpet honeysuckle produces orange to scarlet berries and can climb to fifty feet. Its range is zones 4-9 and it's evergreen in mild climates. Unlike many honeysuckles, it isn't fragrant but it does attract hummingbirds. All honeysuckles are twining vines, so they can climb only what they can twist around.

Silverlace vine, or **fleece vine** (*Polygonum aubertii*), is also known as **mile-a-minute vine** because it can grow fifteen to twenty-five feet in a year and quickly reach a maximum height of thirty to forty feet. It's especially useful for covering a large structure quickly. The upper part of the plant produces showy hanging clusters of tiny fragrant white flowers in late summer. A woody, twining climber with attractive glossy leaves, silverlace vine grows in zones 4-7 and can tolerate shade.

Climbing hydrangea (*Hydrangea anomala petiolaris*) is valuable for many things: its six- to twelve-inch-wide clusters of white summer flowers; its large, handsome shiny dark-green leaves, which nicely offset the flowers; its golden fall foliage; its reddish-brown woody stems, which are showy when the vine is bare; its tolerance, indeed preference, for partial shade; and its ability to climb almost anything (because of its aerial rootlets) and to grow fifty to seventy-five feet high—perhaps more than any other ornamental vine. Climbing hydrangea's range is zones 4-7.

Porcelain vine (*Ampelopsis brevipedunculata*) is named for the glazed porcelainlike finish on its showy clusters of multicolored berries. As the berries ripen in the fall, they become an amazing collection of marblelike red, green, blue, pink, lavender, and purple fruits. The cultivar **'Elegans'** can provide still more color with its variegated green, white, and pink leaves. Porcelain vine climbs rapidly, with tendrils, to twenty feet or more, and it's hardy in zones 4-8. In its tendrils, berries, and coarse-toothed three-lobed leaves—which turn yellow in the fall—it resembles its cousin, the grape.

If you live in a mild-winter climate you can grow many more vines, including several very colorful evergreens. **Carolina jasmine,** or **evening trumpet flower** (*Gelsemium sempervirens*), isn't a true jasmine (see below), but it does produce masses of bright-yellow trumpet-shaped jasmine-scented flowers in late winter and spring. It also has attractive shiny dark-green leaves. Hardy in zones 6-10, Carolina jasmine grows to twenty feet, but it twines only halfheartedly, so it needs support.

Red passionflower (*Passiflora vitifolia*) has striking summer flowers, distinguished by ten long, pointed crimson petals (actually bracts) that remain on the vine after the rest of the flower falls off. Passionflower was named by Spanish missionaries, not for any aphrodisiacal qualities, but because they thought parts of the vine represented the passion, or crucifixion of Christ: the ten bracts signify the ten apostles present at Christ's death and the vine's shiny five-lobed leaves (which resemble those of Boston ivy [*Parthenocissus tricuspidata*]) represent the hands of Christ's persecutors. The intricate white-and-purple flowers of **blue passionflower** (*P. caerulea*) are less striking than the blossoms of the red form. Both plants, however, produce edible deep-purple, plum-size fruits. Hardy in zones 8-9, passionflower climbs with tendrils, so it needs something to twist around.

Mandevilla is a genus of woody vines that are hardy in zones 8-10 and grow slowly to fifteen to twenty feet tall. **Dipladenia,** or **pink allamanda** (*M. splendens*), produces unusually large pink or white flowers from spring to fall. Each trumpet-shaped blossom is two to four inches across and as much as five inches long. The plant's leathery dark-green leaves are big, too—as much as eight inches long. Like Carolina jasmine, **Chilean jasmine** (*M. laxa*) isn't a true jasmine either. But it does bear white, two-inch-wide funnel-shaped flowers throughout the summer, and these showy blossoms have a splendid fragrance. The cultivar **'Alice du Pont'** produces bright pink two- to four-inch-wide flowers from spring to fall.

One of the most colorful vines is **bougainvillea.** From spring to fall it produces masses of often-vivid flower bracts—pink, red, purple, orange, gold, bronze, or white. **Bougainvillea spectabilis** and many of its cultivars grow to thirty feet. **B. glabra** is shorter. Unlike most other vines, bougainvillea neither clings to structures nor twines around them; it must be tied to them. It grows in zones 9-10, but is evergreen only as long as temperatures are above freezing.

Jasmine is celebrated for the delicious, often powerful fragrance of its small white flowers. **Royal jasmine** (*Jasminum nitidum*) is often called **star jasmine** because of its exquisite two-inch-wide blossoms with nine to eleven elegant long pointed petals. The vine is also known as **shining jasmine** because of its glossy leaves. Jasmine blooms almost continuously. **Winter jasmine** (*J. polyanthum*) is named for the fact that its large flower clusters start to appear in February. It's also called **pink jasmine** because its buds and the bottoms of its petals are pink. (To make things even more confusing, it, like royal jasmine, is also called star jasmine.) Both vines are hardy in zones 9-10. **Common white jasmine** (*J. officinale* 'Grandiflorum') is similar to winter jasmine, but hardy in zones 8-10. (*J. nudiflorum* (page 67) is also known as winter jasmine because, like its namesake, it starts blooming in late winter. Unlike other jasmines, however, nudiflorum is hardy in zones 6-10, its flowers are yellow, not white, and they're scentless.) All jasmines grow ten to twenty feet high and, like bougainvillea, they need support to climb.

This long list of colorful trees, shrubs, ground covers, and vines more than amply demonstrates that you don't need high-maintenance perennials or annuals to bring color and interest into your garden. On the contrary, you can actually create *more* color and interest with low-maintenance plants than with labor-intensive ones. There are so many colorful, low-maintenance plants that you could furnish your entire landscape with them and still use only a fraction of the hundreds of different kinds of trees, shrubs, evergreen ground covers, and vines described above.

Perennials and Annuals

If however, you still want to include perennials and annuals in your garden, here are some ideas to help you get the most out of them:

☙ Most perennials bloom for just a few weeks a year; it's their leaves, not their flowers, that you see from spring to fall. Unfortunately, the leaves and stems of most perennials are unremarkable at best. So emphasize exceptional perennials whose foliage is handsome, colorful, or, ideally, both—hostas, for example (see below).

☙ Choose plants with large, long-lasting, and/or prolific blossoms. **Coreopsis** (*Coreopsis* spp.) and **black-eyed Susans** (*Rudbeckia* spp.), for instance, are just two of many tall perennials that bloom for weeks in midsummer.

☙ Only annuals bloom constantly. However, they must be planted annually and watered almost daily, so use them sparingly. To help them make their biggest visual bang, plant them where they'll be most easily seen: in or near the optical center of a space or other natural focal point, where just a few bright flowers will dominate the entire setting.

☙ Remember: Perennials and annuals are herbaceous, not evergreen. The ground where you plant them will be *bare* much of the year. Use them with great restraint, as focal points or accents. Think of them as gemstones in the center of a ring.

Perhaps the most valuable perennials are **hostas.** They're tough; they're hardy in zones 4-10; they thrive even in deep shade; their thick clusters of large, elegant, gracefully arching leaves give them uncommon presence; and many varieties have blue, white, and/or yellow foliage that provides season-long leaf color. So important, in fact, is their colorful foliage that their flowers are virtual afterthoughts.

Perhaps the most striking hostas are the variegated white-and-green varieties whose leaves have the largest areas of white. The foliage of at least three cultivars is as much as fifty percent white. The celebrated *Hosta undulata* 'Medio-variegata,' for example, has beautiful wavy leaves with a big ragged white splotch in the center; '**Night Before Christmas**' and '**White Christmas**' are both named for the enormous white swaths in their foliage. (Other green-and-white hostas—*H. undulata* 'Albomarginata,' for instance—are much less valuable simply because their leaves have much less white.) Other colorful hostas, such as *H.*

sieboldiana 'Elegans,' 'Blue Cadet,' 'Blue Moon' and 'Love Pat,' have blue leaves. 'Blue Wedgewood' and 'Krossa Royal' have silvery blue foliage. '**August Moon,**' '**Fanfare,**' '**Gold Standard,**' and '**Piedmont Gold**' have bright yellow leaves. Pick your favorites. (Photographs, pages 52-53 and 55.)

Unfortunately, hostas are a favorite food of snails and slugs. If you notice leaf damage, you can set small bowls of beer into the earth beside the plants; the beer kills slugs when they slide into it. If you'd rather not empty slug-and-beer-filled bowls (and refill the bowls after every rainstorm), use a chemical snail-and-slug killer.

Other sources of summer-long color are variegated herbaceous ground covers, many of which, like hosta, also do well in shade.

Variegated goutweed (*Aegopodium podagraria* 'Variegatum') has soft, crinkled green leaves with white edges. It's hardy in zones 4-8 and tolerates deep shade.

Dead nettle (*Lamium maculatum*) is a low, fast-spreading ground cover with small, crinkled, heart-shaped leaves. Its variegated cultivars include '**Aureum,**' which has yellow-splotched green leaves; '**Beacon Silver,**' which has striking silvery leaves with green edges; and '**White Nancy,**' which has silvery green leaves. Like goutweed, it's hardy in zones 4-8 and thrives in deep shade.

Lungwort (*Pulmonaria*) also has small, heart-shaped foliage, and it produces small blue, white, or pinkish flowers in the spring. The lovely *P. saccharata* '**Mrs. Moon**' has pretty silver spots on dark-green leaves and small flowers that are pink when in bud but blue when open. *P. saccharata* '**Sissinghurst White**' has white-spotted foliage and white blossoms. Lungwort is hardy in zones 3-8 and can grow in shade.

Heuchera americana '**Dale's Selection**' has attractive purple-blue leaves with deep blue veins as well as white flowers in early summer. Even better is '**Purple Palace,**' named for its wonderful deep-purple leaves, which turn bronzy purple in the fall. Both plants are hardy in zones 4-9.

Persian epimedium (*Epimedium* x *versicolor* 'Sulphureum') has striking deep-red heart-shaped leaves with prominent green veins, as well as delicate white flowers in the spring. It's hardy in zones 5-9 and does well in moderate shade.

Ajuga reptans 'Burgundy Glow' is a rare beauty, with unusual green, white, dark pink, and purple variegated leaves. It has a wide range—zones 3-10—and is most colorful in light shade.

A much taller source of color is variegated **Japanese Solomon's seal** *(Polygonatum odoratum* 'Variegatum'). Like other Solomon's seals, this cultivar can grow as high as two feet, and it has long, pointed leaves and tiny white flowers that dangle below its stems in the spring. Unlike other Solomon's seals, however, its deep-green leaves are edged with striking yellow streaks. Japanese Solomon's seal is hardy in zones 4-8 and can grow in shade.

Spring-to-fall color can also be created by the foliage of several ornamental grasses. The long, delicate, thread-like leaves of **blue fescue** *(Festuca amethystina)* are a stunning silvery blue-green. **Japanese blood grass** *(Imperata cylindrica rubra)* is named for its deep-red leaves. **Variegated bulbous oat grass** *(Arrhenatherum elatius bulbosum* 'Variegatum') has white-striped foliage. The leaves of **manna grass,** or **sweet grass** *(Glyceria maxima* 'Variegata,' also called *G. aquatilis* 'Variegata') have bright-white or creamy-yellow stripes. **Golden variegated hakonechloa** *(Hakonechloa macra* 'Aureola') has lovely bright-yellow leaves with delicate green stripes; in the autumn the foliage is a handsome buff color. Although not technically a grass, the exuberant **variegated Japanese sweet flag** *(Acorus graminius* 'Variegatus') has delicate green-and-white-striped foliage. It's hardy in zones 6-9. All the other grasses are hardy in zones 5-9, except for blue fescue, which grows in zones 4-9.

How to Plant Privacy Barriers

❧ Berms

While berms (see pages 15-27) on large properties can sometimes be built high enough to block views of development by themselves, most berms will need to be planted with evergreen trees or shrubs If your berms need screening plants—and they probably will—you'll have to determine how tall they have to be, what kinds of plants you need, and how many you need for complete privacy.

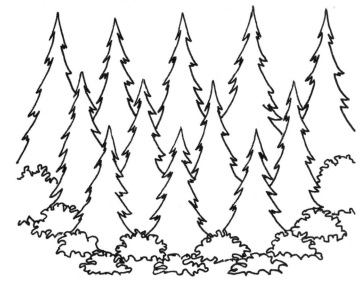

FIGURE 21: *When planting a berm, place the trees or shrubs close enough together to block a view completely. To make the mass look natural, vary the number of rows of plants, so the grouping drifts gracefully up and down the berm.*

If the plants don't have to be more than three or four feet high, evergreen shrubs (see pages 46-48 and 61-63) will suffice. For a higher screen, you'll need evergreen trees (pages 38-40). If the screen must be even higher than any trees you can afford, you'll need evergreen trees that will grow relatively quickly.

Some trees, such as hemlock, grow so thick that just one row may be dense enough to block a view completely, especially if they're planted in enough sunlight. Trees with looser habits—pines, for instance—may require two rows to block a view.

To screen a view completely, install the plants close enough together so you can't see between them. (Don't separate the trees and wait for them to grow together. A privacy barrier delayed is a privacy barrier denied.) If you install the plants in a single row, the branches of one tree should touch, even overlap, those of another. If you plant them in two or more rows, arrange them in a checkerboard pattern (Figure 21).

How to Create Privacy, Color, and Interest . . .

If you need to make the plant barrier as high as possible, install at least one row of plants at the crest of the berm. To make the plants look natural, make the cluster wider and more natural-looking by making it two or more rows deep in some places, and let it drift gracefully up and down the berm (Figure 21).

Plants on a berm that are not needed for privacy—those on a lower slope, for example—don't, of course, have to be placed as close together as plants needed for screening. They can be treated like plants in the Middle Zone (see below).

☙ Hedges

The only difference between berm plantings and privacy hedges is that hedges (see page 27) are planted on a level grade, not on top of a berm, so they must be tall enough, or at least fast-growing enough, to create privacy by themselves. To provide year-round screening, hedges must be evergreen, and the plants must be dense enough, close enough, and numerous enough to create complete privacy. Many of the considerations for planting privacy berms (above) apply to privacy hedges.

☙ Fences, Walls, and Pergolas

Fences, walls, and pergolas (pages 27-28) can all be hidden, softened, and decorated with vines (pages 70-72). Whether the vines are evergreen or deciduous depends upon whether the vine is needed to help create privacy.

If a fence or wall isn't tall enough to provide complete privacy by itself, you can erect lattice on top of it and train an evergreen vine to grow on it. Just like evergreen trees on top of a berm, evergreen vines on top of a fence or wall can make the barrier higher and create still more screening.

If a fence or wall is tall enough to create complete privacy by itself, then vines can be chosen solely for aesthetic reasons. An evergreen vine might still be wanted for year-round interest, but deciduous varieties can also be considered for their fragrance or their colorful flowers, leaves, or berries.

Fences and walls can be hidden and softened not only by vines growing on them but also by trees and shrubs growing in front of them.

If a pergola or other overhead barrier is designed to create privacy (see pages 27-28) you've got to plant it with ever-green vines. If it's designed only to provide shade in warm weather, deciduous vines will suffice. If you want the structure to create shade *only* in warm weather and to let sunlight penetrate it in the winter (to warm your house, for example), deciduous vines are essential.

How to Plant Around Your House

Evergreen shrubs (pages 46-48 and 61-63) are needed around the foundations of most houses for three reasons:

☙ To hide an inherently unattractive concrete foundation (as well as any other unattractive features of the house).

☙ To soften the edges, and especially the corners, of the house.

☙ To give the house a visual base, making it look as if it's a part *of* the site, as Frank Lloyd Wright put it, rather than merely *on* the site.

When installing so-called "foundation plantings" remember:

☙ Make sure the shrubs are high enough, thick enough, and close enough together so none of the foundation is visible at any time, even in the winter. (Only evergreens can provide year-round screening. Lower deciduous shrubs can be planted in front of the evergreen shrubs, of course, but mainly for decoration, not screening.)

☙ Screen any other eyesores—electric or gas meters, wires, faucets, hoses, and so forth.

☙ Plant shrubs far enough from the foundation so they won't touch the house when they grow.

☙ To avoid blocking the view, use lower shrubs under a window (Figure 22). Consider slow-growing and/or dwarf varieties under, especially low windows.

☙ Use larger shrubs at the corners of the house, which is where the contrast between the house and the site is usually the strongest and, therefore, where the building needs more softening than anywhere else along the foundation. (See Figure 22.)

☙ Install shrubs not only around the house proper, but also around the garage and every other building with a concrete foundation and around any other building that needs softening or a visual base.

☙ Foundation plantings can be as extensive as you want.

FIGURE 22: *Foundation plantings should be high enough, thick enough, and close enough together to screen the foundation at all times. Use lower shrubs under windows, larger shrubs at the corners.*

In fact, large groupings of foundation plants are an easy and obvious way to replace high-maintenance grass with low-maintenance shrubs. Deep, layered compositions of shrubs or shrubs and ground covers beside a house can be stunning arrangements. One example: Tall catawba rhododendrons (page 47) can be planted next to the house; shorter P. J. M. rhododendrons (page 47) can be planted in front of them; variegated euonymus (page 48) can be set in front of the P. J. M.s, and vinca (pages 67-68) can be planted in front of the euonymus. The possible combinations are enormous. The more layers of plants you have, of course, the more readily they will hide the foundation.

🍂 Don't prune shrubs into rectangles, squares, balls, or other unnatural geometric shapes. Most shrubs grow into attractive shapes all by themselves. Cut them back only when they're blocking a view from a window or scraping the house or growing into each other and making the whole cluster look messy.

🍂 Don't put wooden "sandwich boards" or other structures over your shrubs to protect them from falling snow and ice in the winter. Those things are usually eyesores. They defeat the purpose of foundation plantings, which, after all, is to make your property attractive. Making your house look a bit like a construction site for three, four, or more months every year just to prevent the possibility of few broken branches is a bad bargain. (Incidentally, ice or snow damage is less apparent on unpruned than pruned shrubs because unpruned plants are looser and more ragged.)

How to Plant the Middle Zone

The Middle Zone of your property is the entire area between your house, which is usually in or near the center of your lot, and the Perimeter. The Middle Zone is the location of every outdoor feature of your home other than foundation

76

plantings and privacy barriers on the Perimeter.

Plants in the Middle Zone don't have to create privacy or hide the foundation of your dwelling. Except for deciduous trees shading your house, their job is simply to create large, colorful gardens comprised of shrubs, trees, ground covers, and vines that—unlike lawns and flower gardens—can be maintained with minimal time and expense.

In general, plants in the Middle Zone should go in whatever space isn't taken up by the lawn, driveway, terrace, or other outdoor amenities.

Like foundation plantings and perennial borders, plants in the Middle Zone should usually be arranged in layers, so each plant can be seen. Put the shortest plants in the front, the tallest in the back, and make sure each plant is taller than the one in front of it.

Layers of plants can be linear—long groupings against a fence, wall, or side of a building, for instance; or along a driveway or walk, or at the edge of a woodland. Layers can also make loops that form planting islands. In planting islands, the tallest plants are in or near the center of the space; the lowest plants are along the edge.

A planting island might have a cluster of dogwoods or other flowering trees in the center, surrounded by mountain laurel, hydrangeas and/or other shrubs, and varieties of vinca and mountain cranberry on the edge. The island could also consist entirely of shrubs of different sizes and types. Or it could be only a grove of trees, or simply one large, shade-giving maple or beech surrounded by winter-creeper or other ground cover. The combinations are limitless.

Layered groups of trees, shrubs, and/or ground covers can be large or small, and they can cover an area of any size, from a corner of a quarter-acre lot to several acres of a suburban mansion. Many Southern gardens, such as Middleton Place, near Charleston, South Carolina, and Airlie, in Wilmington, North Carolina, are planted with vast sweeps of azaleas that make stunning carpets of color in springtime (see photographs, pages 56-57). Responding to one couple's request for an "easy-to-care-for" landscape, the celebrated California landscape architect Thomas Church surrounded their suburban house with a "sea of ivy" broken only by a giant oak, a few shrubs, and curving paths. When two

friends, Myrna and Michael Chen of Goffstown, asked me to "do something" about a scruffy, sandy slope on the north side of their house, I planted it with masses of shrubs—rhododendrons, azaleas, and mountain laurels—that provide color from April to June. My own one-acre woodland garden, Evergreen, consists almost entirely of mature trees and sweeps of broadleaf evergreen shrubs and (mainly) evergreen ground covers (see photographs, pages 49-50 and 53-55). These examples are just a few of many gardens that have been extensively planted with just trees, shrubs, and ground covers.

Properly mulched (see below), tree-shrub-and/or-ground cover plantings require almost no maintenance. Shrub masses are particularly easy to care for because the shrubs hide most, if not all, of the ground behind them. Because the ground inside a shrub mass is out of sight, it needs no ground covers or other plants of any kind; and it needs weeding much less often than the front of the mass because it can be mulched heavily (which inhibits weeds). Any weeds that do appear usually can't be seen. The larger the mass, of course, the larger the area of hidden ground inside it and the greater, therefore, the area of your yard that needs almost no care.

Choosing, Arranging, and Installing Plants

When planting any area of your property, keep these points in mind:

🔊 Some gardening writers say we should avoid some plants—pachysandra, for example—because they have become too "common." Whether or not a plant is overused, however, depends on the characteristics of the plant, not simply how often it's planted. If a species offers lots of color and interest for little effort, it deserves to be popular and probably should be used more often, not less. The only garden plants that are too common are those that demand too much of our time and give us little in return—grass, for instance, and part-time plants such as herbaceous flowers.

🔊 Some gardening writers fret that we're using too many exotic plants and that we should use native species instead—either because aggressive exotics are wiping out weaker native plants and drastically altering the ecosystem or because, they argue, a subdued "natural" garden of "authentic" native plants is somehow better than a garden of exotics. I respectfully disagree with both views. Whatever damage exotic species have done or are doing to the environment—most of which is outside the ambit of residential gardeners—will simply not, for better or worse, be affected very much by how we plant our own homes. Second, landscape design isn't a historic preservation or restoration program, a horticultural equivalent of Colonial Williamsburg, where some plants are preferred simply because they were here first. Landscape design is a meritocracy, where the plant chosen is simply the best plant for the job, regardless of pedigree or national origin. In any case, while gardens can be naturalistic or natural looking, they are never "natural." Only nature is natural. Gardening—all gardening—is artificial, and installing native plants instead of exotic ones doesn't make it any less so.

☛ Too many new (and not so new) gardens consist of a big boring brown sea of bark mulch dotted with a few islands of plants. The plants will grow, of course, and after many years they'll finally cover enough of the bark mulch so the garden won't look so bad. But why wait a decade for a good-looking garden? Beauty delayed is beauty denied. Put plants close enough together so at least two-thirds of the space is green, and stop using mulch as a ground cover. Yes, plants will eventually start crowding each other. But the solution to overcrowding isn't to set plants so far apart that they'll never touch. It's either to prune the plants when overcrowding becomes unsightly or, better, to relocate some of them elsewhere on your property, or give them to a friend or neighbor, or donate them to a garden club sale.

☛ Choose plants that are suited to their site. Make sure they're hardy in your zone and plant them in the proper soil and light.

☛ Plants often have their greatest impact if the same types are grouped in large drifts or sweeps. Clustering plants avoids the all-too-common messy or busy look of too many different kinds of plants crowded into too small a space. Generally, the smaller the plant the larger the sweep must be, for the smaller the plant, the more it needs visual strength in numbers to make an impression. While a very big specimen tree—a giant live oak, for example—looks best all by itself in the middle of a lawn, shrubs usually look better in a group of

at least three or more plants—and often many more (photographs, pages 49-52 and 56-58). (Don't use a pair of the same kind of trees or shrubs in an informal or naturalistic planting; a pair usually suggests bilateral symmetry, and bilateral symmetry connotes a formal garden.) Flowers usually should be arranged in drifts of at least a dozen, and sweeps of low ground covers should usually include several dozen plants (photographs, pages 54-55).

☛ A drift or sweep can rarely be too big (see photograph, page 56, for example). When in doubt, make it larger.

☛ In a planting island or other layered grouping, use just one sweep or drift per layer—one type of ground cover, one kind of low shrub, one type of large shrub, one kind of flowering tree, etc. (One layer, one plant.)

☛ Vary the sizes and shapes of plant groups, especially those within sight of each other. Some groups, for example, might have only three or five shrubs, while some might have ten or twelve, and others, fifteen, twenty, or more.

☛ Large, colorful, or otherwise striking plants can also stand alone or in a small cluster, for variety and accent, often in the middle of a much larger sweep of less colorful plants. In fact, this combination—like a necktie offset by a pure white shirt—is probably the most dramatic way to arrange a garden. The larger, more colorful, or more striking a plant is, and the more it contrasts with the more subdued plants around it, the smaller the number of the colorful plants you need for effect. If the plant is striking enough—a giant specimen tree is the best example—it can stand alone. Using just one or a few bright blooming plants in a prominent position in a large space of more subdued colors was a favorite labor-and water-saving trick of Moorish gardeners in medieval Spain. They knew that just one colorful plant—which needs much less water than a room full of plants—would not be dwarfed by the space but, on the contrary, would dominate it and make the entire area look well planted.

I thought of the Moors when I designed the White and Gold rooms at Evergreen. I created most of the color in the spaces with low-maintenance evergreen shrubs—rosebay rhododendrons and white Emerald Gaiety euonymus in the White Room, and yellow Emerald 'n Gold euonymus in the Gold Room. But I also planted a cluster of white impatiens in the White Room and a container full of yellow coleus in the Gold Room. The annuals need frequent watering, of course, but the watering can be done quickly because there are so few of them. The flowers, however, are so well placed—in the middle of each room, like a large jewel in a crown—that they look ample for the space.. If you use high-maintenance annuals and perennials, follow the Moors' example: Use them sparingly, to get the biggest color bang for your maintenance buck.

☙ You can make trees or shrubs "taller" by planting them in a low planting berm. A two-foot-tall rhododendron atop a two-foot-tall berm is, in effect, a four-foot rhododendron. A modest six-foot maple tree suddenly becomes an impressive nine-foot specimen tree if it's planted on a three-foot berm. And since dirt is cheaper than plants, creating the extra plant height from soil costs much less than creating it from plants alone.

Like privacy berms, planting berms create more than "cheap height." Their hilly forms also make an otherwise level garden more shapely, more three-dimensional, and therefore more interesting. And because berms bring more plants closer to eye level, they make a garden look fuller and lusher.

☙ When installing plants, help them stay moist (and thereby reduce the amount of watering they need) by:

☙ Adding water-retaining peat moss to the back-fill—at least one part peat moss to four parts soil.

☙ Digging shallow wells around plants to catch and hold water.

☙ Spreading two or three inches of organic mulch, such as shredded bark, pine needles, or leaves, around each plant. Mulch is a many-splendored thing. It's so valuable to a low-maintenance garden that you shouldn't even *think* about not using it. Mulch does three things: (1) It helps keep plant roots moist and cool by insulating the soil from sunlight and wind, thus reducing evaporation. (2) It suppresses weeds and makes them easier to pull out when or if they do appear, thereby reducing weeding time substantially. (3) It enriches the soil by adding minerals and humus as it decays, thus reducing (sometimes eliminating) the need for additional fertilizers or soil amendments, such as compost or cow manure.

☙ Let nature give you free mulch—and help you avoid raking—by letting fallen leaves and needles remain around trees, shrubs, and ground covers where they drop. If you find the leaves unattractive, cover them with a thin layer of more attractive organic mulch, such as shredded bark.

☙ Water new plants deeply—that is, with enough water to soak the roots—during the first year they're planted. The larger the plant, the larger and deeper its roots are, so the more water it takes to soak them. The deeper the roots are, however, the farther they are from the surface, so the longer they take to dry out, and the less often they need watering. Newly planted trees and shrubs, for example, need deep watering no more than twice a week—especially if the plant is mulched and peat moss has been added to the soil. Shallow-rooted ground covers and perennials, on the other hand, might need watering three or four times a week, especially in dry weather. If you're lucky and rain waters your plants, you, of course, don't have to.

How can you tell if a plant needs water? Stick your finger in the soil, below the mulch. If the soil feels moist, it doesn't need water. If it feels dry, it does. If it's merely damp, you'd better water, just to be sure.

Unless you derive special pleasure from watering by hand, don't do it. It takes too much time. Either use sprinklers or install an irrigation system. There are pros and cons to either method. Sprinklers are cheaper, of course, but the hoses connected to them are unsightly, and it's a drag to lug them around from watering point to watering point and to coil them up and put them away when you're done. Also, it's hard to move hoses through a garden without damaging any plants. An irrigation system can cost several thousand dollars to install—but it eliminates the hoses, it's easier on your garden, and it reduces your watering time to nothing. My suggestion? Whatever makes you happy. But if you think you want, or might want, an irrigation system, the time to install it is sooner, not later. The longer you wait, the more your garden will grow, and the more damage you'll have to do when you dig it up to install water pipes.

Also remember that trees, shrubs, and ground covers usually need little artificial watering after the first year they're planted, so your watering time should then be minimal. I water my garden only occasionally (during droughts, for instance), and I use hoses and sprinklers because I don't have irrigation. I'm satisfied with the arrangement, however, because the inconvenience is small and I avoided the expense of the irrigation system.

How to Save Time and Money on Your Lawn . . . by Keeping Only As Much As You Need

What's the most popular American landscaping plant? If you said rhododendrons, yews, or junipers, you wouldn't even be close. In fact, if you mentioned *any* shrub, tree, flower, or ground cover you'd be wrong. For the most popular landscape plant by far is grass.

The typical American yard is carpeted, boundary to boundary, with lawn. Yes, there are shrubs beside the house, perhaps a tree or two in front, and some flowers along the walk. But those are the exceptions that prove the rule. The fact is, if anything is growing anywhere in the American yard, chances are better than nine out of ten that that thing is grass.

Part of the reason is economic: Grass is the quickest and cheapest plant to install. A dollar's worth of grass seed—even a dollar's worth of turf—can cover more ground than a dollar's worth of any other plant. That's why, if a contractor landscapes a new house, his planting scheme is usually a few tiny ten-dollar shrubs in front of the house (because the foundation would be ugly-bare without them) and grass—just grass—everywhere else.

When the house is sold, the new owner usually regards his yard as he does the house: as essentially complete. Taking his landscape as a given, he adds little or nothing of his own. Instead he dutifully maintains what the contractor has left him.

And that's too bad. For if grass is a bargain to install it is anything but a bargain to maintain. In fact, the cost of creating a lawn is inversely proportional to the cost of taking care of it. Unlike trees, ground covers, and shrubs, grass is not a native or naturalized plant that largely takes care of itself. On the contrary, a thick, deep-green, weed-free lawn is a highly artificial organism that, in a typical garden, consumes more time and more money—*by far*—than all the other plants combined. Consider the many costs of lawn care:

☙ Watering

Unlike most garden trees, shrubs, and ground covers, grass usually needs watering several times a week in the summer. To deliver that water, you have to install an expensive irrigation system, or you have to water by hand. Even at its easiest, hand-watering usually means schlepping a hose and sprinkler across your lawn, watering one area, coming back in a couple of hours to drag the hose somewhere else, then coming back again, and so on, until the whole job is done.

In the summer, watering a lawn can consume more tap water than any other household function. In the East, as much as one-third of household water is sprayed on the lawn. In dry areas of the West, as much as sixty percent goes on the grass.* An American family can easily spend several hundred dollars a year *just watering the lawn*. And that cost will only rise as an ever-expanding population consumes an ever-greater share of the country's limited water supplies.

Sometimes lawn-irrigation water is unavailable at any price. When a drought dries up a community reservoir, lawn watering is simply banned—and homeowners watch helplessly as their precious, delicate greenswards turn yellow, then brown, after their life-support systems are turned off. Most trees and shrubs will survive a drought unaided—especially if they're mulched (see page 79). But you obviously can't spread a two-inch layer of bark mulch over a lawn. (See Cleaning Up, below.)

☙ Mowing

Unlike any other plant in your garden, lawns need mowing. And, of course, the greener and lusher—i.e., the more attractive—your lawn is, the more mowing it requires. Lawn mowing—which, remember, is just *one aspect* of the care given to just *one part* of your garden—typically takes more time than any other garden chore. One study estimates that Americans spend an average of forty hours a year—or an entire week's worth of labor—cutting grass. If the average

---

* Many statistics on American lawn care can be found in the excellent book, *Redesigning the American Lawn*, by F. Herbert Bormann, Diana Balmori, and Gordon T. Geballe (Yale University Press, 1993).

American adult earns more than $400 a week, then the average American homeowner is lavishing more than $400 worth of labor on his lawn. And that, of course, is only for mowing.

There's also the cost of the mower—at least $100 for a no-frills, push-it-yourself model, at least $200 for a more popular self-propelled machine, and at least as $700 for a ride-on mower. According to the Outdoor Power Equipment Institute, the average American spends $338 for his mower and buys a new one about every seven years, which means he spends more than $48 per year just to purchase a mower.

Power mowers also need regular servicing, including blade sharpening, oil changes, new spark plugs, etc. Even a routine tuneup costs at least $25—and that's when there's nothing wrong with the machine except a dull blade. According to the Outdoor Power Equipment Institute, Americans spend an average of $65 on lawn-mower maintenance every year.

Add in about $5 worth of gas per year, and you can figure that the typical American family spends at least $118 per year just to buy, maintain, and fuel a power mower.

If you hire the work out, your mowing costs will be even higher. The kid next door—if you can get his attention—will probably want at least six or eight dollars an hour for his services. Landscape contractors and other professional lawn-care services will charge three or four times as much. Depending on the size of your lawn, mowing services can easily run anywhere from a couple of hundred dollars a year to several thousand.

Lawn mowing has still other costs. One is noise. Unlike your car, your power mower doesn't have a muffler, so it's probably the noisiest appliance you own. And doesn't at least one of your neighbors like to run his mower at exactly the time you want a little quiet?

Another cost is pollution. Unlike most cars, your mower doesn't have a catalytic converter; according to one study, during every hour it runs it emits as many pollutants as a car driven 350 miles.

❧ Cleaning Up

After a lawn is mowed, you've got to deal with the clippings. Many Americans still rake them up—a chore that takes almost as much time as mowing. Then you've got to dispose of the clippings. A lot of lawn waste is still picked up at the curb and, at great expense, hauled and dumped in landfills—which, in many cities and towns, are rapidly running out of room.

You also have to rake up leaves from your lawn. Unlike grass, most plants—including virtually all trees and shrubs—actually benefit from fallen leaves and needles. This debris creates a valuable layer of organic mulch, which suppresses weeds and eventually decays to enrich and fertilize the soil (see page 79); if trees didn't provide this mulch free, you'd have to provide it yourself. Grass is different. A layer of leaves can kill a lawn, rotting it and/or making its soil too acidic. And even if leaves didn't hurt the lawn, they would still make it all but invisible.

❧ Weeding

Since lawns can't be mulched, they're more susceptible to weeds than virtually any other garden plants. Either you have to pull the weeds out by hand—a chore sometimes as time-consuming as mowing—or you have to kill them with herbicides, whose side effects are dangerous at worst, uncertain at best. Many popular herbicides have been found to be almost as harmful to human beings as they are to weeds. And who knows what we'll find about others—after it's too late.

❧ Liming, Fertilizing, and Other Chores

Unlike many trees, shrubs, and other plants, grass prefers a more neutral soil than the acid soils found in most of the eastern United States. That means you have to spread lime on your lawn once a year and periodically test it for proper pH. Lawns also need fertilizer at least once or twice a year. Some also need aeration and occasional spraying of a pesticide, the effects of which are at least as noxious as herbicides.

Given all the costs of grass, you might think that, far from being our most popular garden plant—the one we grow nearly everywhere—it would be only slightly more welcome than the weeds we try to extirpate from it.

The popularity of grass would be slightly less ironic if it

How to Save Time and Money on Your Lawn . . .

possessed at least one of the features for which we prize other plants—colorful flowers or berries, or handsome evergreen or variegated or unusually colored leaves, or brilliant fall foliage. But grass has none of these things. On the contrary, it's perhaps the least impressive plant in the garden. No other species gives us so little for so much.

What Grass Is For

That's not to say that grass is worthless, however. On the contrary, grass has two valuable properties.

First, it's the only plant that can be walked on regularly without serious damage, the only ground cover that will withstand moderate foot traffic, thus providing a durable planted surface for outdoor activities. Unlike paving, a grass surface is soft, attractive, and cool in warm weather. Grass is essential for croquet, pleasant for volleyball and badminton, and ideal for games like touch football, where a soft surface makes falls less painful and scrapes less likely. Grass is also wonderful for sunbathing and picnicking. Grass also makes lawn parties...lawn parties, and it gives any outdoor living and entertaining a softer, more natural feeling than any paved surface can.

Second, grass paths are cheaper to build and more pleasant to walk on than virtually any paved garden path. Plus, their smooth, horizontal green surfaces make a beautiful contrast to billowing shrubs and other plants beside them. Grass paths can unify a garden by tying it together in long, wide, green ribbons of turf.

But that's it: Those are the only things that only grass can do. In a low-maintenance garden it should therefore be used only where you need what only grass can provide: a ground cover that can be walked on. If you're not going to walk on it (except to mow it)—if the grass will be strictly ornamental—there are literally hundreds of other plants that are much more ornamental and that require only a tiny fraction of the maintenance that turf does. Unless your resources are unlimited, grass simply requires too much care to use it anywhere you don't need it.

On the other hand, don't use grass anywhere you're going to use it too much. Basketball courts and other heavy-duty sports areas, for instance, should be covered with something tougher—a hard paving such as concrete or asphalt, or a soft one such as sand or a sand-clay mix.

When deciding how much lawn you need and where you need it, ask yourself what, if anything, you want to do on it. If the answer is "nothing," you don't need it.

If you *are* going to do something—something that doesn't need a hard surface—then ask yourself exactly how *much* grass you need to do it on.

At Evergreen, we wanted a soft spot just large enough to spread out a blanket for sunbathing. Our lawn is smaller than our kitchen, but it's all the lawn we need.

If you need grass for, say, occasional badminton games, then you'll need a lawn the size of a badminton court. If you plan to play frequently, you'll need a lawn the size of two badminton courts—enough for a second court when you let the first court recover from too much wear. For touch football, you'll want even more grass.

You get the idea. The point is to maintain only as much lawn as you *use* and eliminate the rest.

If you're like most Americans, you probably have more lawn—actually *much* more lawn—than you use.

Do you use your front lawn? If you're like many homeowners, the only time you're on it is when you're maintaining it. (In that sense, it's like an old-fashioned parlor, which, other than to entertain an occasional important guest, seemingly existed only to be cleaned.) If your lawn is like a parlor—if all you do on it is take care of it—get rid of it. Replace it with a berm or other privacy barrier (see Part 1) or with trees, shrubs, ground covers, and other easy-care plants (pages 37-48 and 61-74).

Also eliminate strips of grass too narrow or too steep to use. Any lawn you save should be level, or nearly so. The more level the lawn, the more activities it can be used for—and the easier it is to mow (see below).

Unless you have your own golf course, you should get rid of *any* lawn larger than a quarter-acre. Most people, in fact, don't need—don't use—much more than a sixth of an acre of lawn—about 2,500 square feet, or the equivalent of a 50-foot square. Others—myself included—need less than 400 square feet, or a 20-foot square.

How to Get Rid of Your Lawn

How do you eliminate the grass you don't need?

On most properties, especially those smaller than an acre, the grass near the perimeter can simply be buried under berms. In the Middle Zone, grass can be replaced with groups of trees, shrubs, ground covers, and other plants. If these plants are installed in planting berms (see page 79), the grass will, of course, be buried under them.

If berms aren't used, you can rototill the lawn. By breaking up and turning over the turf, rototilling does two helpful things: (1) It prevents most of the grass from sprouting again because, instead of sprouting, (2) it decays to fertilize and enrich the soil.

You can also kill grass by covering it with black plastic sheeting. The plastic deprives the turf of water, air, and sunlight while allowing the sun to heat the soil. The result: within a year (sometimes sooner) most, if not all, of the grass dies—much of it actually rots away—and the soil is ready for planting. For good measure, you can still rototill the soil before you plant.

Killing grass with plastic, however, has two problems: It takes time, and the plastic is an eyesore. You can cover the plastic with an organic mulch while it's on the ground, but there's not much you can do to speed up the grass-killing process.

A much faster method is to cover the grass with layers of newspaper, then cover the newspaper with topsoil and set out your plants. Covered with dirt, the newspapers will kill the grass, just as plastic will, but newspapers are biodegradable, so they'll eventually rot away.

Still another alternative—one that will ensure that virtually no grass will come back to invade your new plantings— is to dig up the turf and bury it in a berm or throw it on a compost pile. If the grass is especially healthy you can rent a turf cutter, which slices it into long strips, and replant it in another part of the lawn that needs new sod. Digging up turf, however, is hard, time-consuming work. And you may have to add at least some new topsoil to replace the soil you take away with the turf.

However you dispose of your lawn, remember that you can help thwart any surviving grass by spreading at least two inches of organic mulch around the new plants and by adding new mulch every year to replace what rots away (see page 79).

Maintenance Made Easy(er)

If you can get rid of half your lawn—and millions of Americans can eliminate at least that—you can also eliminate half the time you now spend taking care of it.

You can also save time and money by preserving the part of your lawn that's easiest to maintain—healthy, level turf in plenty of sunlight that's relatively easy to mow—and by getting rid of shady, sloping, and scraggly sections that need a lot of work.

You can also save by maintaining your remaining lawn more efficiently. The biggest saving you can make is to stop raking up grass clippings. Leave them on the lawn, where they'll provide a very light mulch, helping the soil retain moisture and reducing the need for watering. As the mulch decays, it'll enrich and aerate the soil and create natural organic fertilizer. Leaving clippings on the lawn doesn't just save you from having to rake them up; it also saves you both water and fertilizer, as well as the time it takes to apply them.

When you leave clippings on your lawn, make them small enough so they disappear into the grass. Thick clumps of clippings left on top of the grass are not only unsightly; they can also harm the grass beneath them. The smaller the clippings, the less they'll hurt the grass, and the faster they'll reach the ground, so the quicker they'll decay.

A so-called mulching mower will chop the clippings up fine enough. But you can dice up clippings with a regular mower simply by running it over them until they disappear. The best way to mow over clippings is to cut the lawn in a continuous circle, beginning on the outside edge and blowing the clippings toward the center. As your circle becomes ever smaller, you'll mow over an ever-smaller ring of clippings, pulverizing most of them and moving the rest toward the middle, where the mower will eventually cut them all up. Just keep mowing over them until you don't see them. To avoid creating too much mulch, mow before you have to cut off more than two inches of grass at a time.

You can also save the cost of buying and maintaining a power mower by buying an old-fashioned reel mower instead. Reel mowers cost only about $100—the price of the cheapest power machines. They seldom need repair (other than blade sharpening). They don't burn gas or oil. They don't pollute. They're better for the lawn than rotary mowers (which is what power mowers usually are) because they cut the grass more sharply than rotary machines and sharper cuts leave grass less susceptible to lawn diseases. Motorless mowers are also safer than power mowers. As anyone over fifty will tell you, they're not much harder to push than power machines (especially on a level lawn), and the newer, lighter models are even easier to push. Reel mowers are also terrific exercise. Since there's no danger of cutting yourself on a power-driven blade, you can even jog behind them (as I like to do), and you can go as fast as you want. Running on a soft, green, fragrant, newly mowed lawn, getting a workout in the fresh air, without having to go to a gym, while getting a chore done at the same time—what more could you want?

The best way to keep weeds and insects out of your grass (thereby reducing the need for pesticides, herbicides, and hand weeding) is to make your lawn as healthy as possible. A healthy lawn grows full and thick, crowding out weeds, and it's less attractive to bugs. Here are several ways to help make your lawn more robust:

❧ Don't cut it too short. Grass two or three inches long shades the soil better than shorter turf, making it harder for weeds to germinate. Longer grass also helps keep the soil moist and produces deeper roots, both of which reduce the need for watering. (Since soil dries out from the top down, the deeper a plant's roots are, the greater the chance that they'll find enough water.)

❧ As with any plant, water a lawn deeply, enough to soak the roots. But don't overwater, as that makes grass susceptible to fungal diseases. An inch or two of water once or twice a week is usually fine. How can you tell for sure? Poke your finger into the ground. If the soil is damp, don't water. If it's dry, water.

❧ Water in the morning, so the grass has all day to dry out. If you water late in the day, the grass may stay wet all night, increasing the risk of fungus.

❧ Fertilize in the spring and fall with an organic fertilizer. Composted cow manure and other organic fertilizers enrich the soil, help decompose thatch (dead clippings and stems), and act more slowly than chemicals, so they give the grass a longer, more consistent dose of nutrients. They're also gentler on the environment because they don't run off into the ground water.

❧ If weeds do appear, try digging them out by hand. If your lawn is both healthy and small, you shouldn't have many to dig. You can shorten your work by concentrating on the most conspicuous and unattractive "weeds" and leaving the rest alone. Use herbicides only as a last resort, and then use only a specific chemical or product for a particular plant in a particular area. Avoid suspected carcinogens.

❧ Avoid pesticides too. They don't kill just grubs and other grass eaters; they also attack "good" insects that eat "bad" ones, as well as earthworms that aerate and fertilize the soil, and microorganisms that break down thatch into fertilizer and enrich the soil at the same time. Happily, pesticides are usually unnecessary. Most healthy lawns can withstand most insect attacks all by themselves.

Finally, don't put metal or vinyl "mowing strips" along the edge of your lawn. Supposedly they make your lawn easier to mow and keep your garden neater by separating your grass from other plants growing next to it. These most unnatural-looking miniwalls are impossible not to notice, though, and they look like a construction material—something you might put up while you were making your garden but would certainly take down before letting anyone come to see it. In other words, "mowing strips" roundly defeat one of their purposes, which is to make a garden more attractive. And if their absence makes mowing take a bit more time, that's a very small price to pay for a better-looking yard.

How to Get the Most Out of Your Land ... by Using What's Already There

Does your property have a woodland? A meadow? Boulders, ledges, or other impressive rock formations? A stream, pond, or other natural water features? A view of mountains or other scenery?

If you have just one of these things you're lucky. For they can be made into some of the most impressive elements of your home garden, often for much less cost than other landscaping.

Rock, water, and other natural features are gifts of nature that can stretch your landscaping dollar. A handsome tree or cascade already on your land is a costly tree you don't have to buy and an even more expensive cascade you don't have to create. Every square foot of your land already covered by an attractive pond, stream, rock, or natural ground cover is space you don't have to landscape. Nature has landscaped it for you. If you have time and money enough to landscape only an acre of your land, for instance, but nature has already landscaped (or nearly landscaped) another acre for you, you'll end up with a two-acre garden, half of it cost free. In gardening, at least, you really *can* get something for nothing. The trick is to use what nature provides.

Gardening by Subtraction

Most landscaping involves mainly *adding* things to the site—berms, plants, etc. When you work with natural features, you begin by taking things away. I call it "gardening by subtraction." Michelangelo said that a statue already exists in the stone; the sculptor simply reveals it by chipping away the stone around it. In the same way, you reveal a natural garden by removing the clutter in its way. This process—gardening by subtraction—includes cleaning up, weeding, and pruning.

Cleaning up is removing any man-made debris from the site, as well as dead wood, including dead, diseased, or dying trees, both standing and fallen, and branches, large and small, lying on the ground.

Weeding is removing any trees, shrubs, and other plants that detract from the beauty of the site.

Pruning is removing unwanted parts of trees, shrubs, or vines.

Gardening by subtraction makes the site more attractive—more like a garden—by removing unattractive debris and clutter that obscures, distracts our attention from, or otherwise blunts the visual impact of the rocks, water, trees, or other, more attractive plants on the site. Gardening by subtraction beautifies a landscape by simplifying and clarifying it.

Many rock and water features don't support trees or shrubs, of course, so they never need weeding or pruning. Ledges, cliffs, boulders, streams, and ponds can usually be made attractive simply by cleaning them up. After they're cleaned up, they'll be impressive focal points and strong organizing elements of a naturalistic garden.

Some special places have already been so well gardened by nature that cleanup alone will make them finished, natural gardens. Among the most notable are ledges fringed by handsome evergreens or carpets of ground covers. You've probably seen many such places, perhaps on or near hilltops with thin soil. Along the rocky coast of Maine, for example, sunny granite ledges are often ringed by large, solid drifts of lowbush blueberry bushes that turn scarlet in the fall. The blueberries are broken only by low pines or spruces, which provide accents and height in the background. The gray ledge organizes the space and perfectly offsets the plants. There is almost nothing a gardener would need to do here—nothing to weed, nothing to plant. Just clean up some errant dead sticks and—voila!—you have a large, handsome natural garden, brought to you virtually without charge by nature.

Other sites, of course, need more work. Some ledges, cliffs, or other large rock features may be surrounded by trees and shrubs that need weeding and pruning. And while ponds and streams usually need only cleaning up, plants along their banks often need weeding and pruning too.

In my garden, Evergreen, low granite cliffs rise dramatically beside a seasonal cascading brook. When I bought the property, a tangle of large honeysuckle bushes growing in and around the streambed hid the water and made the brook almost inaccessible. The lower part of the cliffs, plus some of the brook, were buried under the remains of several large white pines that had been cut down a few years before. When I removed the pine slash, however, the cliffs looked even higher and even more dramatic, because their entire surface was now exposed and there was no clutter to detract from them. And when I pulled up the honeysuckles, it was like pulling a cover away from the brook: Before the bushes were removed, the stream was invisible; afterward, suddenly, almost magically, I could see a long, lovely brook, cascading over mossy rocks. The cliffs and the brook are two of Evergreen's most impressive features (see photographs, pages 59-60). But unlike other parts of the garden, I can take almost no credit for them. For they were gifts of nature. All I had to do was unwrap them.

If you have a stream on your property and that stream has any falling water at all—even a tiny cascade—then nature has given *you* a great gift: an exciting visual and aural focal point that would cost you hundreds, perhaps thousands, of dollars if you had to make it artificially. Waterfalls and cascades are natural fountains. The sound, movement, and radiance of falling water make it one of the most engaging elements in the entire garden. And unlike an artificial waterfall, it doesn't have to be made, doesn't have to be turned on and off, doesn't need electricity to run, doesn't break or wear out, and almost always looks better than a man-made version. All it needs is cleaning up: Once the branches and other tree litter that inevitably fall or flow across it are taken away, there, like Michelangelo's statue, is the falling water: wonderful, shimmering, and perfect, waiting only to be appreciated and enjoyed.

Other valuable natural garden features are large, handsome "glacial erratics," scattered across the land during the last Ice Age. These giant stones are natural sculptures, which can be powerful focal points and organizing elements of a naturalistic garden.

The handsomest, most pleasing stones look like miniature mountains—wide, gently sloping rocks that enter the earth at their widest dimension. These rocks not only look stable and restful, they also appear to be even larger than they really are. You assume that the slope of the rock continues under ground and that the rock above ground is like the tip of an iceberg: a small part of a much larger rock, or even ledge, beneath the earth. The gentler the slope of the rock above ground, the wider and larger you assume the entire rock to be.

If the widest point of a rock is below the ground, you can make the rock "larger" and more impressive by digging dirt away from it. The more rock you can expose, the larger, wider, and generally more impressive the rock will be (Figure 23).

If the widest point of a rock is above the ground, the rock will probably look top-heavy and ungainly. In that case, add dirt around the base of the rock until the ground is as high as its widest part.

Woodland Gardens

If you have a woodland you can transform it into a woodland garden, one of the grandest of all gardens—yet one requiring so little maintenance that it almost takes care of itself (photograph, page 50).

Woodland gardens are impressive because they're vast outdoor rooms whose soaring walls and high ceilings are formed by the tall trunks and leafy crowns of large trees.

Unlike most garden plants, the trees in a woodland garden are free, another gift of nature. And not just any trees, but specimens often so large that they wouldn't be available in any nursery at any price—and would cost thousands of dollars apiece if they were. And that's not all: These trees don't have to be planted. Nature has planted them for you. Plants that take more time and effort to set out than any other plant are already in the ground, growing nicely, waiting for your attention.

Sometimes nature gives you free evergreen shrubs and ground covers as well. In the Northeast, woods may contain stands of mountain laurel. In the South they may have rhododendrons or azaleas. In the Pacific Northwest they may

How to Get the Most Out of Your Land . . .

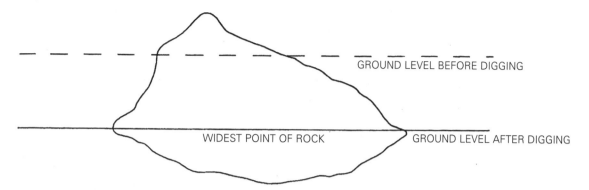

GROUND LEVEL BEFORE DIGGING

WIDEST POINT OF ROCK

GROUND LEVEL AFTER DIGGING

FIGURE 23: *To make a rock as impressive as possible, dig dirt away from it until its widest part is level with the ground.*

have rhododendrons, Oregon grape, or salal. Some woodlands also have handsome ground covers and attractive wildflowers.

One of my clients has a half-acre of mature mountain laurel in his woods. When I first saw the six-foot-high shrubs they nearly covered the ground. I told my client that he was the owner of thousands of dollars worth of shrubs and an all-but-completed woodland garden. All he had to do now was clean out the dead wood, cut some paths among the shrubs, and weed out a few trees to let in more light, so the laurel would bloom better. With just a little gardening by subtraction, he would have an extraordinary landscape, one with a dazzling display of exquisite white blossoms in late spring. And all without having to buy a single plant.

Woodland gardens are unusually economical in another way: Thanks mainly to their trees, they need less maintenance than any other garden I know. They mulch themselves with the thick layer of leaves or needles that fall on the woodland floor. They make their own fertilizer out of decayed mulch. Because they're kept cool and moist by the mulch and the tree canopy, most woodland gardens get most of the water they need from rain or snow. They also need little weeding because the mulch and the tree canopy inhibit other plants. A woodland garden, in other words, is like a forest: a natural ecosystem that takes care of itself. Properly designed, a woodland needs only seasonal cleanup (mainly of dead trees and branches) and occasional watering (mainly during a drought, and then primarily for appearance). No other land-

scape can give you so much garden for so little effort, or so lush a landscape, with so much plant mass—one with so many large trees and shrubs—for such little cost.

A woodland garden has still other advantages: It's a welcome cool place—or at least the coolest place on your property—on a warm day, and a lush, serene, private oasis on *any* day.

To turn your woods into a woodland garden, you begin by gardening by subtraction, making your woods neater, more open, more parklike. Then you lay out paths and add sweeps of shade-tolerant, mainly evergreen shrubs and ground covers along the paths, and a few perennials and annuals for variety and interest. Add appropriate sculpture and furnitur and it's finished. (For detailed, step-by-step instructions ! my book, *The Woodland Garden,* published in 1996 Taylor.)

Borrowing a View

If your property has a view, or potential view, of a mountain or other beautiful natural scenery, make sure you can see it—or "borrow" it, as landscape designers say—so, visually, it becomes part of your garden.

Some properties are so well sited that their views are already visible. On other lots, you may have to cut trees to open up the vistas, to make them wider or deeper, or to make them visible from more vantage points.

A few lots are so large or well sited that everything you see from the property is natural scenery. The views around most

... by Using What's Already There

homes, however, include at least some development. The trick in those cases, of course, is to block views of development (using berms and other privacy barriers, as explained in Part 1) while opening up views of natural scenery. On most lots, in other words, the views have to be carefully controlled.

If, for example, you can see a mountain from your home but also some houses below it, build a berm or other privacy barrier just high enough to hide the houses. If you can see a handsome woodland from your property but you can also see houses to the right and left of it, build privacy barriers to screen just the houses; the barriers will not only hide the unwanted views; they'll also frame the desirable one.

At Evergreen, I cut the lower branches of trees to open up a view of my neighbor's handsome cliffs, but I left the upper branches alone so they would screen houses on top of the cliffs. In other places I built berms to hide neighboring houses, but, where possible, I left openings to "borrow" views of my neighbors' magnificent boulders and pine woodlands.

However you choose to screen your views, the idea is to create the effect of an estate. By opening up every possible view of natural scenery while blocking every view of development, you try to create the illusion that your house is on a large, private, parklike property, surrounded by nothing but undeveloped greenspace.

How to Save More by Building Less: Avoiding Unnecessary Decks, Walls, Driveways, and Steps

Another way to spend less time and money on your yard is by not building unnecessary decks, walls, driveways, and steps. By avoiding, eliminating, or at least reducing the size of this expensive infrastructure, you'll free up money to install privacy barriers and low-maintenance plants instead. Plus you'll have a greener, more natural-looking yard.

Build Terraces Instead of Decks

Wooden decks are expensive to build, and with rising lumber costs they're becoming more expensive every year. They may also be the most difficult part of your property to maintain.

Because nearly all decks are uncovered, they're totally exposed to the weather and thoroughly soaked every time it rains. Much of the deck—the floor—is level, so rainwater lingers until it evaporates. Snow, of course, hangs around until it melts, keeping the wood wet for days or weeks. Especially because decks are usually stained rather than painted, water penetrates the wood and slowly rots it. In cold weather, the water expands as it freezes, literally breaking the wood apart. Damage can be reduced by annual applications of water sealer and stain, but even decks made of pressure-treated wood need regular repairs.

Decks have still other limitations: They can be enjoyed only in warm weather—which, in much of the country, is only a few months a year. And even then they can't be used when it's raining, when it's too hot, or when mosquitos or other insects drive you indoors.

Wooden decks are useful, of course, because they provide a smooth, firm, and level surface for outdoor living. But other surfaces can be smooth, firm, and level too.

A lawn can be as level and almost as smooth as a deck, plus it's softer than wood and, unlike wood, pleasantly cool on a warm day (see page 83). As long as it receives relatively light use—by a just few people for only a few hours a week, for example—grass will remain thick. To avoid wear caused by too many feet in one place (in front of chairs and tables, for instance) you can simply move the furniture to a fresh spot and let the worn turf recover. If the traffic is light enough, you should usually be able to keep your furniture one step ahead of foot wear.

On the other hand, if traffic is so heavy that it wears out your lawn, consider a masonry terrace. A terrace provides a smooth, hard, level surface, just like a deck, but it costs less to build and, more important, it lasts indefinitely, with virtually no maintenance whatsoever. While a wooden deck consists of a floor (or decking) supported by an elaborate framework of posts, beams, and joists, a terrace is a simple structure: concrete, brick, and/or stone paving on a sand, gravel, and/or concrete base.

When building a terrace, you first have to decide where it should go and how big it should be. Its size depends on what you want to use it for and what you want to put on it. Do you want just enough room for one or two people to read or sunbathe? Or do you want enough space for a big crowd and enough chairs and tables to seat everyone? And what about a large barbecue, fireplace, or other features?

Where you build the terrace depends on its use. If it's for entertaining, it should adjoin the public areas of the house, such as the living room. To make food service easier, it should also be as close as possible to the kitchen.

Any terrace, no matter what size, should go in a quiet, private spot and, if possible, one with a good view of your garden or other scenery. If you want it to be in the sun, it should go on the east, west, or, ideally, south side of the house.

The first step in building a terrace is preparing the base. The base—usually crushed stone or gravel—protects the paving from the settling, heaving, and eventual cracking that would otherwise be caused by freezing and thawing water underneath it. Six to ten inches of base, carefully watered and compacted, is usually enough, but it depends on the kind and condition of soil beneath it and on how deep your ground freezes. Building a base is simple, so you can probably do it yourself; but check with a professional in your area to be sure it's deep enough and properly prepared.

After the base is ready, you can install the paving. Your choices include concrete, brick, or stone set in concrete (known as "wet" paving), or brick or stone set in sand (known as "dry" paving). As you may imagine, dry paving is easier for the amateur because you don't have to know anything about working with concrete—a skill that takes a while to master. Also, dry paving is a more forgiving surface because there's no possibility of concrete cracks. The absence of concrete also makes dry paving look more natural.

On the other hand, wet paving is monolithic. There's no settling or heaving of individual bricks or stones; the entire surface stays flat and smooth. Because there's concrete, not sand, between the bricks or stones, the entire surface is hard. It's easier to walk on in high heels, and it's a firm base on which to keep tables level. It's also cleaner than dry paving—and easier to keep clean.

Concrete is the cheapest wet paving, but brick or stone set in concrete are handsomer.

Wet or dry, a masonry terrace is still cheaper than a deck—as one of my clients was surprised to learn. A divorced woman on a slim budget, she told me she wanted to build a small wooden deck behind her house for cookouts, and she was discouraged when a carpenter told her it would cost $2,500. I told her to forget the deck. Instead, I said, spread a load of gravel where she wanted the deck, cover it with two inches of sand, and pave the sand with large flagstones. Instead of a $2,500 deck that would suffer regular water damage, she could have a handsome, maintenance-free terrace for about $400 worth of materials.

Don't Build Unnecessary Walls

Perhaps the costliest gardening mistake is building a retaining wall. They're usually expensive, frequently unattractive, and, worst of all, often totally unnecessary.

The fact is that even a steep slope usually doesn't need to be "retained" by a wall. If the slope were unstable, it would have collapsed long ago. The fact that it's holding is usually a good indicator that it's at the "angle of repose." (As I explain on page 16, that's the angle—usually about forty-five degrees—that earth will assume when it falls freely and comes to rest, or "repose," without any retainer or support.) True, the steeper a slope, the more likely some of it will erode. But erosion can be all but eliminated if the slope is well planted.

Think of how engineers build a nearly level highway through rolling terrain. When they cut the road through a hill, they usually don't build walls to hold up the slope on each side of the road. They simply make a big, V-shaped cut in the earth, making sure the slope is gentle enough to be stable; then they plant grass or other ground cover to prevent erosion. Similarly, when they build a road across a low spot, they dump fill in the depression and build the road on top of it. They don't build walls at the base of the fill to hold it up—they don't have to. They just plant it or cover it with rocks.

The only reason to build a wall is when you have no room for a slope. On small lots, for instance, the space that would be taken up by a slope may be needed for some other use—to make more level land for outdoor activities, for instance (see Figure 24). In those cases, fill must be retained by a space-saving foot-thick wall instead of by a slope that must be at least as wide as the fill is high. Happily, many lots are big enough to have room for both a slope *and* level areas.

So if you have a steep slope on your property and you think you need a wall to hold it back, think again. Probably all it needs—if anything—is more plants.

Suppose, for example, that you want to make a terrace larger by adding fill to the slope below it. You probably won't need to hold up the fill with a wall. Instead, you'll likely have room enough to simply let the fill fall freely. Then you can cover it with loam and plant it with shrubs and ground covers (Figure 25).

Two clients of mine saved about $2,000 by doing exactly that. The space behind their house was too steep for entertaining and other activities. The all-too-common solution to their problem would have been to create one or more terraces by adding fill to the slope, retaining each terrace with a wall, and linking the terraces with steps.

How to Save More by Building Less:

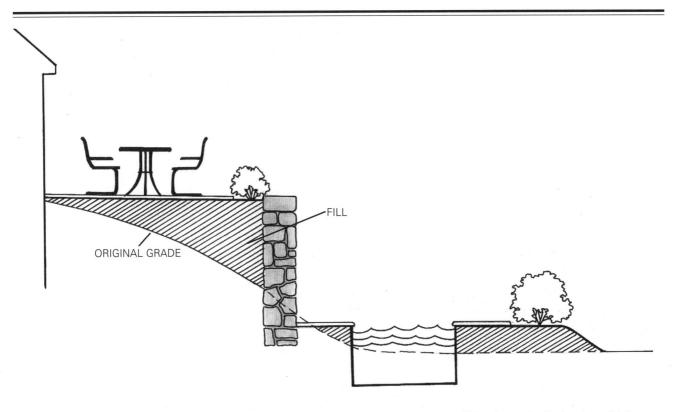

FILL

ORIGINAL GRADE

FIGURE 24: *Retain a slope with a wall only when the property is small and the space that would be taken up by the slope is needed for something else. Here, the space immediately to the right of the newly-widened terrace was needed for a pool.*

I advised the couple to build the terraces and plant them with grass because that was the least expensive and most attractive way to create a level, low-use outdoor activity area (see page 83). But I told them the walls would easily be the costliest and least attractive way to support the terraces. Instead of walls, they would do better to let the fill fall at the edge of each terrace, make the grade slightly more gradual than the angle of repose, add loam to the slopes, and plant them with colorful shrubs. Like the face of a berm (see page 16), the slopes would be an excellent showcase for the shrubs, and they would contrast beautifully with the grass above and below them. Instead of $10,000 walls they could buy $5,000 worth of shrubs that would be large, colorful decorations for their outdoor rooms. They could also save money by connecting their terraces with ramps instead of steps (see page 96).

If you already have a retaining wall, and it's unattractive or needs repair, consider taking it down and letting the soil behind it fall to its angle of repose.

I saved more than $2,000 by taking down most of a retaining wall at Evergreen and made our property more attractive at the same time. Here's how it happened: Our garage is in the basement of our house, so near the garage our driveway is about ten feet below the front yard. To keep the yard from falling into the driveway, an immense fieldstone wall—about ten feet high and twenty-five feet long—had been built between the driveway and the yard. When I bought the house, the wall was starting to crumble and was leaning precariously over the driveway. It was only a matter of time before it crashed onto the driveway—possibly when somebody was walking by.

I could have simply rebuilt the original wall. But that

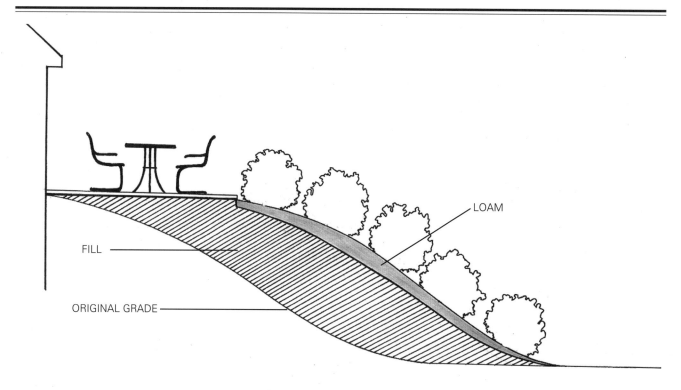

FILL

ORIGINAL GRADE

LOAM

FIGURE 25: *This terrace didn't need to be retained by an expensive wall. It was widened simply by dumping fill on top of the original grade. Part of the fill was leveled to make the terrace larger; the rest was left to fall at its angle of repose. Loam was added to the new slope, and it was planted with evergreen shrubs.*

would have re-created an unattractively large mass of rock wall at a cost of about $5,000; also, the gigantic wall would have hidden many of the plantings in the front yard from anyone walking in the driveway en route to or from our front door. So I decided to rebuild the wall to only about half its original height. With a lower wall, some of the dirt in the front yard did spill into the driveway, and a steep slope was left on top of the wall. But I planted the slope with a Mugo pine, junipers, vinca, ground phlox, and a few other perennials. The plants held the remaining soil nicely, and now from the driveway we see not only an attractive *low* wall but also many plants above it. The steep slope displays the plants in full view, and the handsome gray stone wall makes a rich contrast to the vinca, junipers, and phlox that soften the wall as they spill luxuriantly over the top (see photograph, page 54). What's more, the lower wall cost only $2,800. The better solution was also the cheaper one.

Shorten Your Driveway

Like a lawn, a driveway costs time and money. It has to be patched and resurfaced periodically and cleared of snow and ice in the winter and of leaves and other litter during the rest of the year. More important, driveways usually add nothing to the beauty of a yard. No matter how neat or nicely paved, they're still big slabs of paving (usually asphalt, concrete, or gravel), and no one has ever claimed that they look as good as trees, flowers, or shrubs. Also, driveways usually have cars parked on them and, despite what automobile advertisements would have us believe, cars add no more to a garden than concrete and asphalt. The longer and wider a driveway is, and the more cars parked on it, the more a yard looks like a parking lot and less like a garden.

Obviously, your driveway has to be long enough to reach your garage—if you have a garage and if you park your car(s) inside it. And you surely need someplace to park your vehicles and your guests.' The goal, however, is to make driveways and parking areas as small and unobtrusive as possible. The smaller and/or less visible they are, the less time and money they take to maintain, the greater the ratio of plants to paving in your yard, and the greener and more attractive your property is.

Here are a few ways to make your driveway smaller:

👈 If it's more than one lane wide, and you don't need the extra lane for parking, you can make it narrower. A paving contractor can simply saw off the extra paving and haul it away. (You could also use it as fill in a berm.) Then you can lay loam and install plants where the pavement used to be.

👈 If you have a circular driveway, you can get rid of some or all it. A circular drive lets you pull up to your front door and out to the street again without having to turn around. For that occasional convenience, however, you pay a large and continuous price: Your whole front yard is bisected by a strip of paving at least ten feet wide and fifty feet long. Its focal point is a giant semicircle of pavement with perhaps a car or two on top for emphasis. Instead of a garden, your front yard is a well-landscaped linear parking lot.

Most houses with a circular driveway have another driveway going to the garage, as well as a side door to the house that's usually close to the garage. If the circular driveway were removed and replaced with a walkway from the garage driveway to the front door, the owner would lose so little and gain so much. Yes, he'd now have to turn around before driving into the street (or back directly into it), and he'd have to walk a few feet farther to get to his front door. But he could also drive up to the garage and enter the house from the side door—which many people routinely do anyway. More important, his front yard would be free of exactly the kind of intrusion that berms and other barriers are intended to screen.

One client complained to me that her home had no outdoor living space. She was right: Her backyard was private, but it was just a long, narrow hallway-size corridor along the crest of a steep slope. Her front yard was a spacious lawn, but it was almost never used because it was sloping, totally open to the street, and broken up by a wide concrete circular driveway.

The lawn, however, sloped toward the house, and this facilitated a wonderful solution to her problem. I told her to tear out the driveway and, in the lower two-thirds of the slope, carve out a roughly semicircular level area and plant it with grass; this would make a commodious outdoor living room. The fill removed from the semicircle could be used to build a berm on the upper third of the slope. If the berm were planted with evergreen shrubs, the lawn would not only be screened from the street, it would also be embraced by a high semicircle of flowering evergreen shrubs. There was another bonus: The entrance to the house, near the center point of the semicircle, was framed by a large, handsome porte cochere. If the driveway were removed, the structure would become both a grand open garden house furnished with classic outdoor benches, tables and chairs, as well as a handsome garden focal point, planted with clematis, wisteria, and other flowering vines.

Save Unnecessary Steps

Some people can't resist building steps on even the gentlest slope. And that's a pity. For steps are often unnecessary, and they have three major disadvantages:

👈 Like decks and walls, they're expensive to build and maintain.

👈 Steps, especially informal, irregular ones, are often more difficult to negotiate than level paths because you've got to look down when you walk on them. As Frederick Law Olmsted wrote, walking in a garden should be effortless, requiring no thought about what's under your feet. Only when walking is effortless can all your attention go to the plants around you, and nothing interfere with the pleasure of the garden. The unhappy irony of steps is that they're intended to make walking the garden easier but often make it harder.

👈 Steps are out of place in a naturalistic garden. No matter how "rustic" they are, they still look man-made. Both looking at and walking on them make the garden seem less natural.

Most residential lots are nearly level and need no steps other than those at entrances to the house. (And sometimes even those can be avoided. See below.)

Other lots may have gentle slopes, grades that rise at an angle of less than five degrees from level grade. On these properties, sidewalks may consist of level or nearly level stretches broken by steps. But the steps are often unnecessary. Instead of climbing intermittently and sharply on steps, a walkway could climb steadily and gradually on a gently sloping, ramplike grade, which is easier and more pleasant to walk than a level grade interrupted by steps.

Several years ago we had to repair the approach to our guest apartment. Sections of the concrete walkway had settled into the ground, and a single brick step leading to the brick entrance landing was crumbling. The most expensive solution was to rebuild both the walkway and the step. A slightly less expensive solution was to build a new walkway and a concrete step; the concrete step, however, would clash with the brick landing. An even less expensive solution—and the one we adopted—was simply to slope the walkway up to the height of the old step, which made a new step unnecessary.

Some properties have hillier grades where at least a few steps are unavoidable, especially on steep slopes and at front entrances. But in other parts of the yard there are usually alternatives.

A path, for instance, doesn't always need to climb a steep slope. It can go around, across, or along the bottom of it. In fact, paths at the bottom of a grade tend to make a more attractive garden. For the lower a path is, the higher the trees and shrubs beside it appear to be, and the lusher the garden looks as you walk through it.

If a path does have to climb a steep slope—to reach a viewpoint, for instance—it usually doesn't need to go directly up the bank. Instead, it can go diagonally *across* it, like a hiking trail traversing the slope of a mountain. If the slope is long, the path can zigzag, like switchbacks on a hiking path or hairpin turns on a mountain road. A path that meanders up a slope is less steep than one going directly to the top. Also, because the path takes longer to walk, the garden experience lasts longer, and the garden seems larger and fuller when you stroll through it.

If you need to lay a path across a steep slope, you may have to make a shelf in the slope so the footing will be level. If the ground is relatively root free, you can level the path by a simple process known as "cutting and filling." To do that, you dig, or "cut," into the hillside on the up-slope side of the path, then use the soil you've removed to raise, or "fill," the down-slope side (see Figure 26).

Sometimes the ground is rooty and can't be readily dug. In those cases it may be easier to level the path simply by bringing in new fill to raise the down-slope side.

Sometimes you may have to build a path down a steep slope that's too narrow for a diagonal or switchbacking path, or simply too steep or rough for *any* path. But even then the solution isn't necessarily steps. It's often an earthen ramp.

An earthen ramp is a very simple structure. It's just fill dumped on the bottom of a steep slope to make the grade gentle enough to walk up or down on without steps (see Figure 27). A ramp replaces a precipitous grade with a more gradual one.

An earthen ramp has several advantages:

🖝 It's faster, cheaper, and easier to build than steps or a concrete ramp.

🖝 Because it's dirt, it costs virtually nothing to maintain, unlike masonry and especially wood.

🖝 Because it's earthen, it looks natural, unlike steps or wooden or concrete ramps.

🖝 A ramp demands less concentration to walk on than steps, so it interferes less with the enjoyment of the garden.

To build an earthen ramp, simply dump fill (usually an equal mix of sand and clay) at the bottom of the steep slope until the grade is gentle enough to ascend and descend comfortably. Make the top of the ramp at least two feet wide, enough for one person to walk on easily.

To make the ramp look natural, make it irregular—slightly curving instead of straight, wider in some places, narrower in others—and vary the grade of the slopes on either side of the path. Cover the slopes with loam and plant them, and cover the top, or walking surface, of the ramp the same way you would surface any other path in your yard.

How to Save More by Building Less:

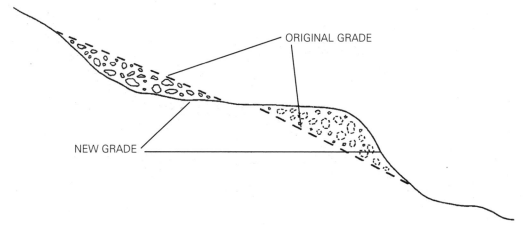

FIGURE 26: *You can level a path on a hillside by "cutting-and-filling." "Cut" fill from the up-slope side of a path and use it to "fill" the down-slope side.*

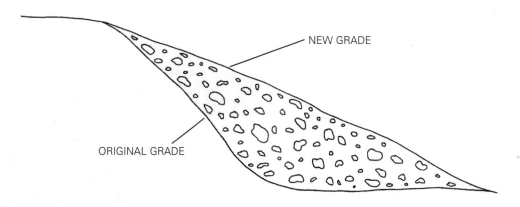

FIGURE 27: *You can make a path up a slope gentler by building an earth ramp, which is nothing more than fill dumped at the bottom of the slope.*

I f you can't build a ramp—and you're very sure that you need to route a path straight up a steep slope—then, and only then, will you need to build steps.

If you do, make them harmonize with the site as much as you can. If the steps are near your house, and if your house is brick, stone, or dark-stained wood, you can build them out of the same material as the building. (Make sure both the colors and textures of the materials match.) If the steps are away from your house, they should fit the character of the garden.

In an informal, natural garden, the best material is usually stones that look like other stones on the site or in your region. The larger the stones and the more irregularly they're arranged, the more natural they'll look.

Logs look less natural than stone because, while stones may be found on the ground in your yard, logs are probably not. Also, their sawn ends look highly artificial—because they are (there are no saws in nature). Also, logs rot, and they're slippery when wet. If you have to use them (or already have them), make sure the sawn ends are covered with dirt, so they can't be seen.

Bricks and smooth, square-cut stone are out of place in the naturalistic garden because they're not found in nature and their straight lines, square corners, and smooth, flat planes clash with the irregular curves, rough surfaces, and soft textures of the informal garden. Concrete—another obviously man-made material—should be used only to bind stones, and as little as possible should be visible when the job is done.

Man-made straight lines, flat planes, and square corners are fine in a formal garden, so steps can be made of brick or of granite, bluestone, slate, or other smooth-cut, right-angled stone.

Landscape timbers should usually be avoided in any garden. They're too rough for a formal garden, too artificial-looking for a naturalistic garden (they're sawed not just at the ends, like logs, but on all sides), and, like all wood, they require too much upkeep for low-maintenance landscaping. If you already have landscape-timber steps in your garden, you can soften their impact by covering the ends and as much as possible of the risers, and even some of the treads with dirt and plants.

One of my clients built a handsome cottage on top of a steep bluff beside a small lake. He planned to build several retaining walls to control erosion, plus a 130-foot-long flight of wooden stairs from his cottage to the lakeshore.

I told him he didn't need any walls. What little erosion there was could easily be controlled by shrubs and ground covers, and the plants were needed anyway to add color and interest to a rather bare slope.

I also told him that the stairs would be a bit of an eyesore, costly to build and maintain, and that most of them were unnecessary. I explained that many parts of the slope were gentle enough so that, with just a little fill, I could build a path that would switch back and forth down more than two-thirds of the bluff. I also suggested planting sweeps of shrubs and ground covers along the path, so the trail would not only be a low-cost, low-maintenance route to the lake, but would also be part of a large, graceful stroll garden on the sunny slope in front of his cottage. The only stairs he needed was a short flight over an especially steep pitch at the bottom of the bluff. So instead of spending $10,000 or more on walls and $3,000 on stairs (and more money rebuilding them later on), he had to spend less than $1,000 on stairs and about $800 on a path, thereby freeing up literally thousands of dollars to buy shrubs, ground covers, and perennial flowers.

I've urged you to avoid decks, walls, and steps whenever possible for mainly one reason: to save money for more important things: privacy barriers and extensive plantings. Aesthetically there is nothing intrinsically wrong with decks, walls, or steps. On the contrary, properly designed, they can add drama, beauty, and elegance to many gardens. Similarly, there is nothing aesthetically wrong with vast lawns, sweeps of annuals, and other traditional labor-intensive gardening. My point is not that they're not beautiful; it's that they're not necessary—that there are less expensive but equally effective ways of creating beauty, utility, and privacy.

Getting Started

Now you're ready to start work. You have to determine:

☛ Where you need privacy barriers on your Perimeter; how tall they have to be; whether they should be berms, hedges, or fences; how much space they'll take up; and how they'll be planted.

☛ What low-maintenance trees, shrubs, and ground covers you want in the Middle Zone and exactly where they should go.

☛ How many and what kinds of evergreen plants, if any, you need to add to screen the foundation of your house and how they should be arranged.

If your property is typical you'll probably have just two major things to do: building and planting a berm along your Perimeter and replacing any lawn you don't need with trees, shrubs, and ground covers. On many properties both projects can probably be done at the same time. Because many lots are now almost entirely planted with grass, anything built on them—including a berm—will automatically bury any turf underneath it. If the berm is planted with trees, shrubs, and ground covers, it will create privacy, it will obliterate a large chunk of high-maintenance lawn, and it will replace the grass with colorful low-care plantings—all at the same time!

On smaller lots, in fact, many if not most of the trees and shrubs will be on berms, because berms will take up much, if not most, of the space available for plants. The remaining land—mostly the Middle Zone—will be filled up by outdoor amenities, including whatever lawn is left for recreation, entertaining, and other uses.

The larger the property, of course, the smaller the proportion taken up by berms, the larger the Middle Zone, and the more room left for ornamental plants.

When you plan your landscape, you won't need to make elaborate drawings that take hours to prepare. Rough sketches are fine. In fact, it's quicker, easier, and much clearer to indicate your plans not on paper but on the ground, with stakes and surveyor's tape. The colored tape (sold in most hardware stores) can indicate the boundaries of berms, planting islands, and other features. Stakes can show the location of each tree and shrub.

However you plan your garden, remember the wisdom of Frederick Law Olmsted. Plans, he reminded us, are only a rough design of a landscape, and they reflect the ideas of the designer only at the moment they're drawn. The best gardens are designed not only before they're built, but as they're being built. For a design can and should be refined and improved as the work progresses, both because the designer changes his mind—presumably for the better—and because improvements become obvious only after the garden starts to exist on the ground.

U.S.D.A. Plant Hardiness Zone Chart

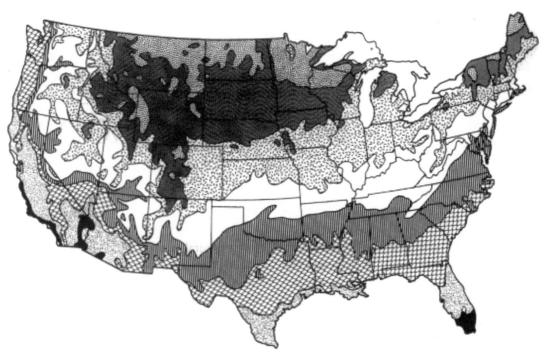

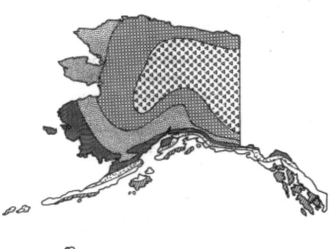

RANGE OF AVERAGE ANNUAL MINIMUM TEMPERATURES FOR EACH ZONE

	Zone 1: Below -50°F
	Zone 2: -50° to -40°
	Zone 3: -40° to -30°
	Zone 4: -30° to -20°
	Zone 5: -20° to -10°
	Zone 6: -10° to 0°
	Zone 7: 0° to 10°
	Zone 8: 10° to 20°
	Zone 9: 20° to 30°
	Zone 10: 30° to 40°
	Zone 11: Above 40°

Index

About the author

Robert Gillmore is a nationally recognized landscape designer, author, and lecturer.

He is perhaps best known for Evergreen, his naturalistic one-acre woodland garden at his home in Goffstown, New Hampshire, and for his pathbreaking landscaping book, *The Woodland Garden* (Taylor, 1996). The renowned garden writer and former *New York Times* gardening columnist Allen Lacy hailed *The Woodland Garden* as "an excellent and much-welcomed guide to building a low-maintenance, naturalistic garden in the woods."

Now, in another seminal work, Gillmore explains how, with berms and low-maintenance plantings, homeowners with small lots and small budgets can create both the privacy and extensive gardens usually found only on very large properties.

Gillmore, 54, was graduated, cum laude and with honors, from Williams and received his Ph. D. from the University of Virginia, where he was a du Pont Fellow.

He can be reached at Box 410, Goffstown, New Hampshire 03045; telephone 603-497-8020.